TRAINING
SOURCES

Faultless Facilitation

TRAINING
SOURCES

Faultless Facilitation

book of activities

LOIS B HART

Viva Books

New Delhi | Mumbai | Chennai | Kolkata | Bangalore | Hyderabad | Kochi

First published as "Training Activities: Faultless Facilitation"

This edition published in 2009
Reprinted 2010

VIVA BOOKS PRIVATE LIMITED

- 4737/23 Ansari Road, Daryaganj, New Delhi 110 002
  E-mail: vivadelhi@vivagroupindia.net, Tel. 42242200
- 76, Service Industries, Shirvane, Sector 1, Nerul, Navi Mumbai 400 706
  E-mail: vivamumbai@vivagroupindia.net, Tel. 27721273, 27721274
- Jamals Fazal Chambers, 26 Greams Road, Chennai 600 006
  E-mail: vivachennai@vivagroupindia.net, Tel. 28290304, 28294241
- B-103, Jindal Towers, 21/1A/3 Darga Road, Kolkata 700 017
  E-mail: vivakolkata@vivagroupindia.net, Tel. 22836381, 22816713
- 7, Sovereign Park Apartments, 56-58, K. R. Road, Basavanagudi, Bangalore 560 004
  E-mail: vivabangalore@vivagroupindia.net, Tel. 26607409, 26607410
- 101-102 Mughal Marc Apartments, 3-4-637 to 641, Narayanguda, Hyderabad 500 029
  E-mail: vivahyderabad@vivagroupindia.net, Tel. 27564481, 27564482
- Beevi Towers, First Floor, SRM Road, Kaloor, Kochi 682 018, Kerala
  E-mail: vivakochi@vivagroupindia.net, Tel: 0484-2403055, 2403056
- 232, GNB Road, Beside UCO Bank, Silpukhuri, Guwahati 781 003
  E-mail: vivaguwahati@vivagroupindia.net, Tel: 0361-2666386

www.vivagroupindia.com

Published by arrangement with

Kogan Page Limited
120 Pentonville Road
London, N1 9JN, UK

ISBN: 978-81-309-1059-8

Published by Vinod Vasishtha for Viva Books Private Limited, 4737/23, Ansari Road, Daryaganj, New Delhi - 110 002. Printed and bound by Raj Press, R-3, Inderpuri, New Delhi - 110 012.

M0000 / M0453

Contents

Chapter 1

Getting Ready to be a Faultless Facilitator

INTRODUCTION

Are you someone who recently went to a group meeting and was 'volunteered' to lead the group yet you have never facilitated a group before?

Are you someone who, along with some other employees, was selected by your manager to begin facilitating a Total Quality Management team and you wish you could first get some training?

Are you about to take up a new position as a trainer and would like to be absolutely confident about your facilitation skills?

Are you someone who has always been interested in how groups function, and therefore feel that if you could learn more about facilitation you might be able to offer your skills to your organization?

Are you someone who already has been facilitating a group or a team, perhaps a trainer, but have run into some problem people who are disrupting the group's process?

Faultless Facilitation was written for all of you. In my work as a consultant and trainer, I meet many individuals who are anxious to learn more about facilitation. I also meet managers who want to capitalize on the skills of certain employees and teach them how to be facilitators.

Both types of people are frustrated by the lack of useful resources to show them how to be successful.

This book will help both managers and employees. Chapter 2 will clarify exactly what I mean by facilitating and facilitation.

The material in this book is based on my individual consultation and facilitation training programme. The content is comprehensive and ranges from the administrative details of setting up a room to the more involved steps for using various problem solving methods.

This is a reference guide organized so that you can quickly refer to the information you need at a particular moment.

Effective facilitators are always trying out new ideas. They are experimenters and risk takers. So don't be afraid to explore the methods you read about in this book.

Effective facilitators also know there are no absolutes – that what works in one circumstance may not in another. Therefore, as you try out ideas found in this book, take notes on what worked and what you'd do differently next time. Adapt these ideas to fit your style and what you know about your group members.

You're on your way now to becoming a Faultless Facilitator!

WHAT DO YOU ALREADY KNOW ABOUT FACILITATION?

You probably already know a lot about facilitating a team of people and it is important to give yourself credit for this prior experience and knowledge. In addition, you must assess what else you need to learn about facilitation so that you can use this book's resources to develop yourself further.

The purpose of this assessment is for you to review your past experiences, your motivation for becoming a facilitator, what skills you already possess and those you need to develop.

1. EXPERIENCES AS A FACILITATOR: List any experiences

you've had as a facilitator of any group including those at work and in your community.

Star (*) the ones that were most satisfying to you and identify why.

2. MOTIVATION: Why do you want to be a facilitator?

3. BENEFITS: How will you benefit from learning more about facilitation?

4. RESPONSIBILITIES: Do you currently have any responsibility for facilitating a group or team? If yes, describe your group: what stage they are in, what is working and what is not working for you as a facilitator of that group.

   If no, are there any groups or teams that you could facilitate in the near future? Describe.

The following is a list of skills and methods that will be presented in this book. As you read over this list, rate your current level of competence and confidence in each one. Make notes to yourself on any of these skills.

1 = I have no knowledge or experience in this area.
2 = I have some knowledge or experience in this area.

3 = I can do this at an average level of competency.
4 = I am confident in this area.
5 = I feel competent and confident enough to teach someone else.

_____ The difference between leading, training, and facilitating
_____ The role of the facilitator
_____ Roles people play in groups and teams
_____ Handling problem people
_____ The role of the recorder
_____ The role of a process observer
_____ How to use outside resource people
_____ Setting up arrangements for a group meeting
_____ How to warm-up a group or team and get them started
_____ How to get a group or team to make a commitment
_____ Guidelines for giving feedback
_____ How adults work together
_____ Observation of non-verbal signals
_____ Listening and paraphrasing
_____ Asking questions
_____ Mediating conflicts between people
_____ How to regroup creatively
_____ Determining timing
_____ How to keep energy flowing
_____ Using the brainstorming technique
_____ Using the nominal grouping technique
_____ Using a force field analysis
_____ How to reach consensus
_____ How to use the problem solving method
_____ How to use a flipchart
_____ How to use a videotape or film
_____ How to use transparencies
_____ How to prepare a presentation
_____ How to write summary reports
_____ Ending the group's or team's experience
_____ Evaluating how well the group or team worked together

Chapter 2

Understanding Leadership and Facilitation

INTRODUCTION

The self-assessment that you completed in Chapter 1 gave you an overview of the skills involved in effective facilitation.

As you begin learning and practising these skills, it is important to clarify what certain terms mean. Words like *team* and *group* may seem interchangeable, but they mean different things to different people. This is also true of the words *leader* and *facilitator*.

Teams go through some predictable stages of development just as human beings do.. As a facilitator, you need to be able to identify the stage your group is at so that you can adapt to the members' needs.

There is also a difference between *training* and *facilitating*.

Chapter 2 defines these terms and outlines leadership and group development models which support the other information found in this book. Part of your responsibility as a facilitator will be to explain these terms and models to your team or group.

WILL YOU BE FACILITATING A GROUP OR A TEAM?

Getting ready to be a facilitator first requires you to identify who you will be facilitating.

You will, of course, be working with other people, but in what context? Will you be working with a group of people or a team of people?

A group is a number of people who are gathered closely together and form a recognizable unit. A group requires three or more people who are located in close proximity. Others outside this group will perceive them as a distinctive entity.

For example, there is a group of doctors who work in the same medical centre whom the public identifies as a part of that centre. Or, there is a group of middle managers who all work in a particular company in the same building. Or, there is a group of human resource directors who all belong to the same professional organization.

But what is missing is the element of purpose. Once we add a purpose to a group's existence, then we are starting to form a team. Team members work together on a common goal, mission, vision or purpose. Teams succeed at doing something; they don't just exist. They want to improve performance, solve a problem, or tackle some issue.

A team is a complex entity, not simply a group of people. An effective team deals with leadership, communication, organizational structure, work procedures and interpersonal relations.

A team is a highly developed group which has learned how to work together to achieve its goals. It focuses on the process by which it will function. Team members explore possible methods of working together, try out those methods, then revise and refine them.

The purpose of this book is to show you how to facilitate a **team** of people.

LEADING *v.* FACILITATING

Is there a difference between leading and facilitating a team? Yes and no.

The leadership model developed by Kenneth Blanchard* suggests that the effective leader always diagnoses the needs of the followers so the leader can help them get their work done.

* Blanchard Training and Development, 125 State Place, Escondido, CA 92026.

The leader then adapts his or her leadership style to fit one of four changing situations or phases. More specifically, Blanchard suggests that the leader adapts his/her style of leadership in two areas: the amount of direction and the amount of support provided. This adaptation is influenced by the followers' level of competence and commitment to the task.

So initially, when a follower is low in competence but high in commitment to the work, the leader is highly directive. Next, the leader moves into a coaching role when this follower has gained more skills and confidence but still may need support. Third, the leader moves into a supporting role when the follower demonstrates competence to accomplish the job and is generally committed and motivated. In the last phase, the leader's role is one of delegating because the follower is coping well for most of the time.

A leader usually works with a team of people, so the challenge for any leader is to adapt his/her style to meet the changing needs of several people at the same time. The key to effective leadership, then, is to accurately diagnose the needs of the individuals in the team and to adapt one's leadership to fit those changing needs.

The focus of this book, however, is on facilitating a team of people who are working together on a common purpose. So we need to apply the leadership model to a group setting.

Groups predictably go through stages, just as individuals do. R.B. Lacoursiere* outlines five stages of group development:

1. **Orientation:** when the members are new to the group, they are probably both anxious and excited and yet unclear as to why they are together;
2. **Dissatisfaction:** when reality does not live up to earlier expectations;
3. **Resolution:** when the members resolve conflicts between them-

* R.B. Lacoursiere, *The Life Cycle of Groups: Group Developmental State Theory* (New York: Human Services Press, 1980). Available through Blanchard Training and Development.

selves, focus on common goals, increase their skills and feel more committed than ever before;
4. **Production:** when the tasks are getting done and the relationships are functioning well; and
5. **Termination:** when the group disbands.

Just as a leader needs to diagnose the needs of the individuals and adapt his or her style to fit those needs, the leader of a team must also be a good diagnostician and flexible to the changing status of the group. In stage one when a group first forms, that's all it is – a group of people. The leader will need to use activities and methods that will help the group develop its vision or purpose.

In stage two, as the group loses some of its initial excitement, the leader will need to provide more support to the members, develop their skills, and refine the vision.

In stage three, the leader helps the team to fine-tune its processes as they take more responsibility for what happens in the group. They are moving towards a '*self managing*' mode so the leader pulls back control and encourages them to take charge.

As the team demonstrates its ability to be highly productive in stage four, the leader steps back more and becomes just a member of the team, providing direction and support only as needed by the group members.

A wise leader continues the diagnosis of the group's accomplishments relative to its original purpose while introducing the idea that the group's life may be reaching an end. This is both a happy and sad occasion for any group of people who have gone through a great deal together. The leader needs to prepare them for this inevitable transition.

Until now, you have learned about the relationship between a leader and his or her followers or team. The question still remains: is the role of a leader different from that of a facilitator?

In this book, we will be using the word *facilitator* for the person who leads a group or team of people. We use facilitator because it connotes involvement in a group whereas a *leader* works both with individuals who are functioning at diverse tasks and also with a group which is trying to achieve a common goal.

The facilitator holds the key role in a group so that it accomplishes its goals and tasks. Facilitation makes sure that things get done more easily; thus, when done properly, the facilitator eases a group through the process of solving a problem, making a decision, redefining its goals, or restating expectations and responsibilities.

FACILITATING *v.* TRAINING

Before moving on, however, there is one more key distinction to be made. It revolves around the difference between a facilitator and a trainer. The distinction between the two roles is one of the relationship between the content and process used.

Someone who trains, instructs or teaches has some specific content that needs to be presented, practised and learned by participants. An effective trainer prepares objectives, a design, exercises and activities that introduce and reinforce the content, and some means of testing to assure that the new skills and knowledge have been learned. The trainer must also pay attention to the process, evaluating whether the planned activities are in a meaningful, properly paced sequence and whether the participants interrelate well.

A facilitator's role is different from a trainer's because the focus is primarily on process. The facilitator must know the group members' attitudes, commitment, skills and experience. The content of the group's experience is the group itself. Its objective is to accomplish its chosen goal. Thus the facilitator does not have a set design but must instead have many methods and techniques available to use with the group as it goes through the five stages of development. The majority of this book covers these important facilitation methods.

Chapter 3

Playing Different Roles in a Group or a Team

INTRODUCTION

Now that you have basic terms defined, you are ready to learn about the different roles people play in groups and teams.

Facilitators hold certain attitudes and use certain behaviours in their role, which are outlined in this chapter. The 'recorder' is the support person for the facilitator, so this role is also outlined. There are examples of how to introduce these two key roles to the members.

A third key role is that of the process observer who silently observes the group or team's process and gives feedback on these observations. Included are several forms a process observer can use.

Organizations use facilitators in one of three different ways. Reviewing these possible uses will help you to assess in which of these ways you will be used as a facilitator.

Group and team members play a variety of roles. Two types of role are outlined: those that relate to getting the task accomplished and those that have to do with maintaining the team's process.

Often you will encounter some members who hinder the process and you will need to learn how to deal with these problem people.

The last part of this chapter covers the effective use of outside resource people. Explain the team's goals and be specific about your reasons for requesting assistance.

THE FAULTLESS FACILITATOR

The facilitator has the key role in a group so that it accomplishes its goals and tasks. As the dictionary suggests, to facilitate is to make something easier; thus, when done properly, the facilitator eases a group through the process of solving a problem, making a decision, redefining its goals, or restating expectations and responsibilities.

As you prepare to facilitate staff meetings, team development groups, or training sessions, keep in mind what your role will be as their facilitator. Generally, these are the key attitudes and behaviours you will need while functioning as a facilitator:

REMAIN NEUTRAL – Remain neutral during the meeting because your role is to facilitate the group's process. If you have valuable ideas or opinions that are essential to what is being discussed – and this happens frequently during the process – put your facilitator role aside and ask someone else to act as the facilitator while you give your input.

KEEP THE FOCUS – Keep the members' focus on the group's common task, problem or issues while at the same time observing how the group works together.

BE POSITIVE – Serve as a positive force in the group, setting the tone so that the very best solutions can be found. You must resolve any doubts you have about any issue the group will be discussing so you can leave your own negativity behind.

ENCOURAGE PARTICIPATION – Encourage participation by all group members by monitoring any excessive talkers and prompting the quieter members. Confront other problem behaviours that interfere with the group's process.

PROTECT IDEAS – Always protect individuals and their ideas from attack by other members of the group. This is a basic ground rule that everyone is asked to follow.

DO NOT EVALUATE – Do not evaluate the ideas that are suggested. Instead encourage the contributors to explain the background behind their ideas.

SUGGEST METHODS – Suggest alternative methods and procedures that will help the group to make a decision. You will need to know how to use some essential methods such as brainstorming, nominal group technique, consensus, negotiating and force field analysis. The goal is to use whatever methods are necessary so that the group comes up with a satisfactory solution.

PREPARE A RECORDER – Since you will be busy facilitating, find (and train if necessary) someone who'll be your recorder so that a group record can be kept and distributed later to the group members.

EDUCATE THE MEMBERS – Observe the roles various group members play and the effectiveness of the methods they are using to resolve problems and make decisions. Share your observations with them. This helps to educate them as to how they could better work together and get their tasks accomplished successfully.

COORDINATE DETAILS – Administratively, you may also have to coordinate the pre- and post-meeting logistics of selecting and setting up the room, sending out announcements, and arranging for equipment and refreshments.

PREPARE A REPORT – Both the group members and your boss will need a record of what happened in each group meeting. Make sure this is done either by you or by the recorder.

Throughout this book you will find more detailed explanations on how to develop these key facilitation behaviours.

Introducing the Facilitator's Role and Responsibilities

Whenever you start out facilitating a group, it is important to spell out clearly your role and responsibilities to the group members. This is also necessary if you are switching from a previously directive role to a facilitative one.

The purpose of doing an introduction is to clearly define your role and responsibilities and the roles the other group members might be asked to play.

Here is a sample introduction you could adapt to fit your situation:

'Hello, my name is ____________ and I'm going to be your facilitator.

My role is to help you to focus your energies on the task. I am going to try hard to remain neutral. I will always defend you from personal attack. Just so that we're all clear; being a facilitator means that I am not going to impose my ideas on you or evaluate what you contribute.

'I'll make some suggestions, but mostly about the process we will use in this meeting, methods we can perhaps use to make decisions or ways we can improve participation. I'm here to help you accomplish your goals.

'Being a facilitator is difficult. I've been trying to learn more about how to facilitate and will be applying what I've learned as I work with you. Please bear with me and let me know if you think I've stepped out of my role.

'With your help, we'll have a productive meeting and get a lot accomplished.'

THE RIGHT-HAND - THE RECORDER

The recorder serves as the right-hand assistant to the facilitator. The role of the recorder is to create the group's record of what participants say throughout the group process. This recording provides a visual tool or instant replay of what is happening.

When recording is done properly, the facilitator and group members are freer to concentrate on the agenda, productivity of the group is increased, and accurate records are kept for future reference.

Who Should Be the Recorder?

There are three ways group members become recorders. Sometimes the facilitator selects one or asks for a volunteer. In some groups, the members rotate this role.

If a recorder is selected before the meeting starts, there's time for reviewing the procedures with the recorder. If you ask for volunteers at the beginning of the meeting, be sure to ask for those who have performed this role before.

Groups that meet regularly often rotate this role among the members so that everyone shares the work and can participate more fully when not serving as the recorder. This is also good training ground for moving into a facilitator's role.

Three helpful characteristics of a recorder include someone whose handwriting is legible, someone who can write quickly and, if a flipchart is used, someone who is comfortable standing up at an easel while writing.

The Recorder's Role

Review the following outline of the role and its responsibilities with whoever will serve as the recorder:

SUPPORT THE FACILITATOR – As the recorder, you serve as the right-hand assistant to the facilitator. The two of you are a team, so clarify your roles before the meeting, watch for ways you can support the facilitator (such as handing out papers), and periodically ask the facilitator if there are other ways you can be helpful.

REMAIN NEUTRAL – Your job is to record, therefore you need to remain as neutral as possible during a group discussion. If you have ideas or opinions that you feel would help the group, ask permission to add your input.

LISTEN, THEN WRITE – Concentrate on what each person is saying before attempting to write it down. Listen for key phrases and words. If they aren't clear, paraphrase what was said.

DO NOT EVALUATE OR EDIT – You are to neither judge nor interpret what was said because this will discourage contributions.

WRITE BRIEFLY – Even though you shouldn't edit, if what is said is too wordy, write down the essence of the idea. Sometimes you'll need to suggest a succinct phrasing, but it's best to ask the person speaking.

RECORD ON EITHER A FLIPCHART OR LARGE PAPER – It helps if the recording is done in front of the group so that they can see what has been said and refer to key points. See Chapter 7 for more tips on using a flipchart.

CONTROL THE PACE – If you fall behind with your recording, stop the group until you catch up. If too much information is being generated (during brainstorming, for example), ask another person to help record on a second flipchart.

Introducing the Recorder

Just as it is important to introduce the role of the facilitator, the recorder's role and responsibilities also need to be defined to the group members. Here's a sample introduction you can adapt to fit your situation:

> 'Hello, my name is ____________ and I've been asked to assist our facilitator by serving as your recorder.
>
> 'I'm going to record what happens in our meeting on this flipchart (or paper posted on the wall). Obviously I can't write down everything so I'll try to catch key ideas using your words. Please let me know if I miss something that you think is important or if I start to editorialize what you said. I may make my own interpretations so keep me honest. If I get too far behind, I'll ask you to wait a moment until I catch up. If you can't read my writing, let me know. And oh, I'm new at this and a little nervous, so if I misspell a word, please consider it my creative licence!'

THE QUIET OBSERVER

Although the facilitator is always observing what is happening in the group, it is hard to keep track of everything that occurs. Therefore, consider adding the role of a process observer occasionally. This would be filled by one member of the group. This frees the facilitator from having to observe everything and adds an additional perspective on the group process.

This quiet observer is just that. He or she sits quietly, a little apart from the group, and takes notes on what is observed.

It is a good idea to introduce this special role to the total group and suggest that members take turns being the observer. Explain the value of paying attention to the group's process and then receiving feedback, so that the group continues to learn and develop.

Always give the observer something to observe. Forms for the process observer are found in various places in the book:

1. Examples of open-ended questions are found on page 25. You and the observer can develop your own set of questions that fit what has been happening in the group.
2. Noting the interactions between group members is a method described on pages 26–7.
3. A form for observing the task and maintenance behaviours of group or team members, both the helpful and hindering behaviours, is found on page 32.
4. When you want to observe the facilitator helping the group or team to reach consensus, use the form on page 106.
5. An observer can note how a facilitator uses the key communication skills of listening with the form found on page 74 and of the questioning skills on page 80.

Regardless of which form is chosen, ask the observer to sit a little apart so that he or she isn't tempted to get involved in the discussion and notes can be taken more privately. The observer could also be a timekeeper if that would be helpful.

When the segment of the meeting being observed is complete, the observer shares what was observed with the rest of group. Be sure to remind the observer (and the group) of the rules for giving feedback (which are found in Chapter 4).

End with asking the observer what was easy or hard about playing this role so that he or she learns from the experience and will want to do it again.

QUESTIONS FOR THE OBSERVER

Atmosphere

1. Watch for evidence that describes the general atmosphere in the group, especially whether cooperative or competitive, friendly or hostile.

2. Did the atmosphere change? If yes, what caused the shift?

Participation

1. Who participated the most?

2. Who participated the least?

3. What was happening in the group's process that helped or hindered participation?

Commitment and Synergy

1. Indicate any evidence of group commitment and synergy.

2. When, if ever, did energy and interest lag? What was happening at the time when this occurred?

PATTERNS OF INTERACTIONS IN GROUPS

From this perspective, the process observer records who communicates with whom, not the discussion content or the members' roles. This perspective will help the facilitator identify persistent or underutilized networking channels.

There are four common patterns of communication in groups, although many more exist. The first three patterns record only person-to-person interactions.

1. RECITATIVE – like a classroom interaction
   - Communication originates from or is directed toward one person
   - Has different reasons for centring – high status, aggression, expert, controlling leader
   - May be legitimate if temporary
   - Probably unhealthy if continual

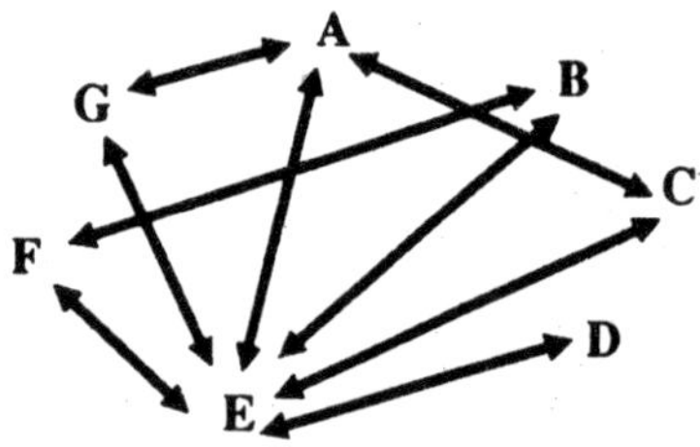

2. SUBGROUPING – private conversations
   - Takes members out of discussion
   - Splits attention of the group
   - May occur because of too little interest in the topic
   - May occur because of great interest in the topic

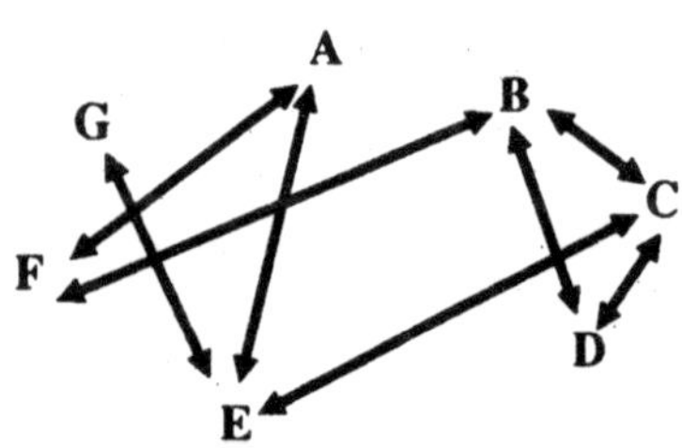

3. DIALOGUE – public subgrouping
   - Usually a process of a dispute
   - Is like watching a tennis match
   - Other group members may become apathetic
   - Healthy if short term

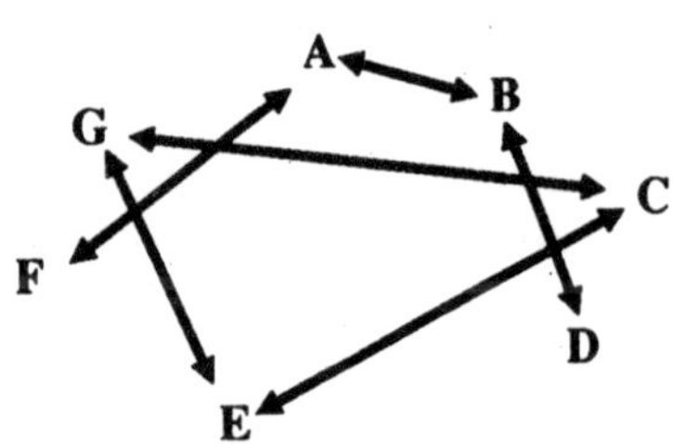

In the fourth pattern, the process observer also records group-directed remarks.

4. MULTILATERAL – free-flowing communication
   - Centring of attention is random and free-flowing
   - Group-centred comments predominate
   - Openness invites all members to participate

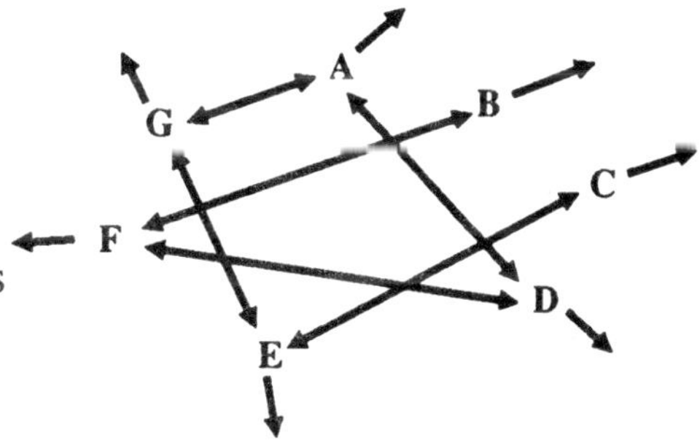

THREE WAYS TO USE FACILITATION SKILLS

Various organizations use their facilitators in one of three ways: (1) the leader is the facilitator; (2) the facilitator supports the leader; or (3) the facilitator works alone. Review these three ways and assess which way you are currently using your facilitation skills. Does this fit your organization's needs? Also, consider different ways you can help your organization by using all these skills.

The Organizational Leader Uses Facilitation Skills

Often, organizational leaders who are concerned about how their groups are working will decide that they want to learn more about leading them. They will seek out resources and training programmes on team development, facilitation, and leadership.

These leaders retain their authority over their staff or team but make the effort to improve their ability to facilitate the progress of their group and thus achieve their goals.

What is difficult about the leader using newly acquired facilitation skills is that group members usually retain their previous perceptions of their leader. So if this leader decides to move into a more facilitative role, the group will have to shift those perceptions.

If you are such a leader, once you learn facilitation skills, explain this shift in roles to your group or team. State your concerns, outline what you have been learning about leadership and facilitation, and elicit their support and commitment. Also, outline what roles they can play in this process, such as recording and observing.

The Supporter of the Leader

In some organizations, a group of employees is selected and trained in facilitation skills for the purpose of supporting the organizational leaders. In this case, the leaders retain their authority and conduct the meetings.

The supporter reinforces the leader's efforts and activities. Often, the supporter is the process observer, noting what is helping or hindering the group's process. The supporter can be the recorder and the time keeper. Regularly or periodically, the supporter can meet with the leader to evaluate what's working and make suggestions as to what needs improving in the process the leader is using.

Using a separate person in this supportive role can be confusing to the group members so if you add this role, be sure to explain the purpose to the group and outline exactly what this person will and won't be doing.

This role requires trust between the leader and the supporter. The leader cannot be threatened by the presence of an outsider or the feedback this person may give. The supporter must be alert in making observations and assertive about giving feedback to the leader and group members.

The Facilitator Who Works Alone

Many organizations train their employees to be used whenever and wherever they are needed to lead a group. Often they facilitate an *ad hoc* group that has formed to solve a specific problem so this facilitator stays with them as their leader until that problem is resolved.

Sometimes, one of these 'floating facilitators' is called in to help staff who are trying to work out some procedural or personality problems. The facilitator is objective but takes charge to see the staff through finding some resolution. During this process, the actual leader becomes a member of the group.

These facilitators also work well during a retreat where visions are created, goals established or re-evaluated. Since retreats usually run for a day or longer, the facilitator may initially lead the group. Later on, the actual leader may take over while the facilitator moves into a supportive role.

The group members and management must trust the facilitator and agree to accept this objective role. If you plan to facilitate this way, make sure you get support from your managers and that they clearly explain the purpose of using an outside person and what role the leader and facilitator will play.

Working alone as the facilitator requires training and confidence. You must be prepared and flexible. You need to be highly observant and assertive when you think the group needs to try something out or hear some frank feedback.

GROUP MEMBERS WEAR MANY HATS!

Members of any group will assume a variety of roles and as a facilitator it is important to recognize them. These roles fall into two types: roles that relate to getting the tasks accomplished and roles that have to do with the maintenance of the group's process.

As you can see on the following chart (page 31), there are six key roles in both the task and maintenance categories. When these roles are assumed by group members, the productivity of the group increases. For instance, individuals who initiate ideas, seek or give information, clarify or summarize and suggest how the group might be reaching agreement, are helping the group accomplish its goals.

Or there may be individuals who encourage others to participate, who speak for the group's needs, who seek ways to keep communication open and resolve conflicts, who offer compromises and check that procedures are being used properly. They also help the group to accomplish its goals and maintain healthy relationships among the members.

Unfortunately, there are roles that other individuals may display that will impede the group's process, such as criticizing others, stubbornly sticking to their own ideas, dominating the process, acting up, withdrawing or avoiding tough issues.

One of the tasks of a facilitator is to be able to recognize quickly the roles people are playing, so study the following chart carefully.

Next, take the chart and the observation worksheet that follows it to a group meeting in which you are a participant. Following the directions on the observation sheet, note who is demonstrating each task and maintenance role. Do this as many times as you need in a variety of meetings until you can readily recognize these key roles.

Although most people are aware of their predominant traits, they may not realize how their characteristics may either help or hinder their colleagues in their group. Another part of the role as a facilitator is to bring this information to the attention of these individuals and even to the whole group.

Those individuals who act out the hindering roles become a problem to the facilitator and the group. Techniques for dealing with them are discussed in the section 'Handling Problem People' (page 36).

Group members should periodically be praised for the roles they play that help the group function. As the facilitator, incorporate time during the meeting to compliment individuals on the helpful roles they have played. More formally, this information can be shared when the group's progress is reviewed (as outlined in Chapter 10 under 'Evaluating Your Group').

ROLES PEOPLE PLAY IN A GROUP

HELPING ROLES: THOSE WHICH INCREASE GROUP PRODUCTIVITY		HINDERING ROLES: THOSE WHICH IMPEDE GROUP PROGRESS
TASK ROLES	MAINTENANCE ROLES	
1. INITIATING: Proposing task or goals; defining a group problem; suggesting procedure or ideas for getting the task accomplished. 2. INFORMATION OR OPINION SEEKING: Requesting facts; seeking relevant information about a group concern; asking for suggestions, ideas or opinions. 3. INFORMATION OR OPINION GIVING: Offering facts; providing relevant information about group concerns; stating a belief; giving suggestions, ideas or opinions. 4. CLARIFYING: Interpreting or reflecting ideas and suggestions; clearing up conclusions; indicating alternatives and issues before the group; giving examples; defining terms. 5. SUMMARIZING: Pulling together related ideas; restating suggestions after group has discussed them; offering a decision or conclusion for the group to accept or reject. 6. CONSENSUS TESTING: Checking with the group to see how much agreement has been reached and how ready the group members are to consider a decision.	1. ENCOURAGING: Being friendly, warm, and responsive to others; accepting others and their contributions; regarding others by giving them an opportunity to contribute or be recognized. 2. HARMONIZING: Attempting to reconcile disagreements; reducing tension; getting people to explore their differences. 3. EXPRESSING GROUP FEELINGS: Sensing feelings, mood, relationships within the group; sharing own feelings with other members. 4. GATEKEEPING: Helping to keep communication channels open; facilitating the participation of others; suggesting procedures that permit sharing remarks. 5. COMPROMISING: When own ideas or status are involved in a conflict, offering a compromise which yields status; admitting error; modifying ideas in interest of group cohesion or growth. 6. STANDARD SETTING AND TESTING: Checking whether the group is satisfied with its procedures; suggesting new procedures when necessary.	1. DOMINATING: Asserting authority or superiority to manipulate the group or certain members; interrupting contributions of others; controlling through use of flattery; patronizing. 2. WITHDRAWING: Removing self psychologically or physically from the group; not talking; answering any questions briefly. 3. AVOIDING: Changing the topic; uncomfortable with conflict; frequently absent. 4. DEGRADING: Putting down others' ideas and suggestions; deflating others' status; joking in a barbed or sarcastic way. 5. UNCOOPERATIVE: Disagreeing and opposing ideas; resisting stubbornly the group's wishes for personally oriented reasons; using hidden agenda to thwart group progress. 6. SIDE CONVERSATIONS: Whispering and having private conversations across the table with another person.

OBSERVING TASK AND MAINTENANCE ROLES

Record your observations of the task and maintenance roles that are seen in the group. Record them on this chart. The left-hand column lists task and maintenance roles. Place the names of all group members along the top of the page. As you observe pertinent behaviours, make a tally or make notes in the appropriate column.

GROUP MEMBERS' NAMES							
TASK ROLES: 1. Initiating							
2. Information or opinion seeking							
3. Information or opinion giving							
4. Clarifying							
5. Summarizing							
6. Consensus testing							
MAINTENANCE ROLES: 1. Encouraging							
2. Harmonizing							
3. Expressing group feelings							
4. Gatekeeping							
5. Compromising							
6. Standard setting and testing							
HINDERING ROLES 1. Dominating							
2. Withdrawing							
3. Avoiding							
4. Degrading							
5. Uncooperative							
6. Side conversations							

YOU'RE WORKING WITH ADULTS!

Getting off on the right foot includes setting and maintaining an appropriate attitude towards your group members. You will be working with adults who learn, grow and interact differently from children. Therefore, it is important to keep in mind key adult learning principles as you facilitate groups of adults.

If you follow these principles, you will increase the likelihood of your group members being committed to the group's goals faster and generating more solutions to problems.

First, compare how children *v.* adults approach a group experience:

CHILDREN	ADULTS
Have little or no experience upon which to draw – are relatively 'clean slates'	Have much past experience upon which to draw – may have fixed viewpoints
Have little ability to serve as a knowledgeable resource to other classmates	Have significant ability to serve as a knowledgeable resource to the facilitator and group members
Focus on content	Focus on problems
Less actively involved	Expect high participation
Rely on others to decide what is important to be learned and done	Decide for themselves what is important to be covered in the group
Accept the information being presented at face value	Need to validate the information based on their beliefs and experiences

Expect what they are doing will be useful in the long-run	Expect what they are doing to be immediately useful
Work in an authority-oriented environment	Function best in a collaborative environment
Assume that planning is the facilitator's responsibility	Share planning with the group members and facilitator

APPLYING ADULT LEARNING PRINCIPLES TO FACILITATION

The differences between how children and adults learn and work demonstrate the need for some specific principles to be followed when working with adults in groups. Use this checklist of nine principles to establish your attitude. Periodically, evaluate your attitude towards them.

DO I . . .

- Encourage them to determine their goals and plan the agenda?
- Relate the group activities to their goals?
- Help them to focus on 'real world' problems?
- Draw upon their past experiences?
- Encourage full participation?
- Allow debate and challenge of ideas?
- Listen to and respect the opinions of group members?
- Encourage members to share resources with each other?
- Emphasize how they can apply what happens in the group?

HANDLING PROBLEM PEOPLE

All facilitators, even the most experienced ones, occasionally have to deal with problem people and situations. Problem situations are those in which the group process is affected by the behaviour of one or more of the group members.

On page 32, there was a chart of task and maintenance roles that people will assume in a group. The third part of that chart outlined six roles that hindered the group's progress. Let's review these problem people and their impact on the group's process. Later, we will look at how to overcome these problems.

Too Much or Too Little Participation

When group members are actively involved and participating in the process, then the group's goals are more likely to be accomplished. The facilitation skills you have been using should encourage this desired group participation. Frequently, however, problem situations have to do with the level of participation of group members.

Some differences in levels of participation are a natural outcome of people's personalities. The extrovert could dominate any group process and the shy person may be more withdrawn. Thus a problem occurs when there is too much or too little participation.

The domineering or too talkative person interrupts, goes on and on with his or her own ideas or experiences and generally controls what is happening. Naturally other group members may not be able to participate fully. Time may also run out before everything is completed for that session. Over-talkative individuals may simply be very enthusiastic and excited about what is happening in your group, and you'll need to harness this energy.

At the other end of the spectrum, the withdrawn or silent individual can also cause a problem because his or her input is hidden from the group. It is also difficult to assess what they are getting out of the group experience. Silent individuals may just be nervous about expressing themselves in front of the group.

Avoiding

When there are unresolved conflicts, hidden agendas or tough issues, people who dislike conflict will want to avoid what they perceive as unpleasant. However, these conflicts and issues must be addressed if the group is ever to accomplish its goals. Some avoiders solve the problem by not even attending the meeting, or by coming late or leaving early.

Degrading

Another type of person criticizes others' ideas and suggestions, either in a joking or a condescending way. This problem must be nipped early on as, otherwise, other group members will feel inhibited and not participate out of fear of becoming the debunker's next victim.

Uncooperative

These people block the group's progress by objecting to ideas and proposed solutions with comments that are totally out of order or unreasonable. Usually they stubbornly defend their position. They may interrupt a lot. Like the avoiders, they may come late, leave early, or not come at all.

Side Conversationalists

When two people lean over and engage in a private conversation, this can be not only disconcerting to the facilitator but also interrupt the group's process. Even more disruptive are two people (or more) who start a second conversation across the table.

Dealing with These Problem People

When the group process is inhibited or affected by any of these problems, you must take action before there is a negative impact on the group.

There is always more than one alternative to try when there is a problem, so you will need to think about your choices before acting. There are three criteria to keep in mind when determining how to handle these problem situations:

1. The goal is to eliminate or minimize the behaviour. The problem needs to be at least minimized so that the group can continue functioning.
2. You need to take care of the problem in a way that doesn't reduce the self-esteem of the individual exhibiting the problem behaviour.
3. Avoid further disruption of the group's process. You need to preserve a climate that is relaxed, comfortable, and conducive to the group process.

Identifying Some Alternatives

As a facilitator, it is tempting to feel that perhaps you caused the problem or that the problem behaviour is a reflection of hostility towards you. It is important to remain as emotionally neutral as possible so that you can identify the best alternatives for handling the situation.

One way to do this is to use this three-step model to identify and select the best alternative for the situation.

STEP 1: Identify possible alternatives – those you have seen other facilitators use as well as those you think would fit the situation. Do not limit your list.

STEP 2: Evaluate these ideas against the three criteria discussed above, eliminating those that do not meet all three conditions.

STEP 3: Select an alternative to use in handling the problem situation.

The following are a few suggestions on how you might deal with each of these six problem people. As you think of other ideas, add them to this list for future use.

The Dominator or Excessive Talker

- Establish a procedure in which each person contributes one idea to the topic being discussed and must then wait until every other group member does the same before contributing again.
- Interrupt the person who is rambling, ask him or her to summarize the point quickly so that the others can add their ideas too.
- Say, 'Thank you for giving us all of those ideas. Let's hear from the others in the group now.'

The Withdrawn or Shy Person

- Do some warm-up activities when the group first starts to work together and occasionally thereafter. This should help even the quietest person to feel more comfortable with the other group members.
- Talk to this person privately. Find out what he or she is thinking and feeling and ask how he or she would like to participate.
- Direct questions to this person when you know he or she has experience or ideas on the topic.

The Avoider

- Do not let conflicts remain unresolved. Keep the group working on problems and tough issues until solutions are found.

- Direct questions to, and solicit ideas from, the avoider so this person stays involved.
- Talk to the avoider privately to find out what's happening.

The Degrader

- When your group first gets together, review your contract and ground rules with them. These guidelines should include the rule that all ideas will be accepted. The very first time someone criticizes another person, this rule must be reinforced. To maintain the self-esteem of the degrader, you may need to do this in private.
- Confront the degrader by saying, 'You may have a point, but we need to solve our problem.'

The Uncooperative

- Incorporate statements in the original guidelines that deal with cooperation and interruptions.
- Encourage this person to explain reasons behind his/her objection. Look for any aspect of the position that supports the group's ideas so that this person moves towards the majority view.
- Refocus his/her participation as a recorder or process observer.
- Ask the group to deal with this uncooperative behaviour.

The Side Conversationalists

- Set guidelines and expectations at the beginning of the meeting.
- Stop the meeting and ask those involved in the side conversation to share with the group what they are talking about.
- Stop the meeting and comment that it is difficult for you to hear the

other discussion or to concentrate on the topic at hand with side conversations occurring.

- Privately talk to the distractors and discuss their expectations for the meeting's topics. If they are different from what is being covered at this time, suggest that they could leave and return to a session that includes their topics. Or suggest that they wait patiently and quietly until the topics arise that they need to discuss.
- Empower others to confront the distractors with how these side conversations keep everyone from concentrating on the group's discussion.

BRINGING IN RESOURCE PEOPLE

There are times when your team might need to invite a resource person to your meeting so they can help the group achieve their goals. An uninvited and unprepared outsider can disrupt your group and be a problem for you as the facilitator.

First, clarify why you need an outside person to visit your group or team. Inviting an outside resource person serves some important purposes. Look over this checklist of possible reasons to determine if it is time to bring in a resource person. Confirm your reasons with your group or team members.

Which of the following addresses your reasons for bringing in a resource person?

______ Has expertise in a particular topic and can provide background information on the problem being addressed by your team?

______ Needs to hear what the team's been doing so that the proposed plans can be compared with those of the organization?

______ Will provide a different perspective on the problem?

______ Has had experience with the problem at hand?

______ Will motivate you and the group members?

______ Will lend credibility to the team's efforts?

______ Will be able to suggest additional resources?

______ Will validate what the team is doing?

Second, once you know why you need an outside person and have made your selection, you need to confirm details thoroughly. You are the link between your team and him/her so do the following:

_____ Confirm the date, time, and place of the meeting.

_____ Give a profile of the team members.

_____ Give an overview of the team's goals and activities so far.

_____ Explain the reason(s) you need this resource person's presence.

_____ Outline when he/she will do a presentation within the meeting.

_____ Designate any time restrictions.

_____ Confirm whether he/she needs any supplies or equipment.

_____ Confirm all of these details and expectations in writing. Provide a map, parking permit, organizational literature and your phone number.

Third, decide how to introduce your resource person so your group members are clear as to the purpose of this visit.

Fourth, send a thank-you note and any follow-up report.

Chapter 4

Getting Off on the Right Foot

INTRODUCTION

Getting off on the right foot includes both coordinating many details beforehand and planning warm-up activities.

The first section in this chapter covers administrative details. Coordinating the arrangements for group and team meetings requires attention to many details, which are outlined on several checklists in this chapter. These include a general list of tasks and checklists for selecting a site and for evaluating the meeting room. There is also a plan of five ways to arrange a room and a list of supplies and equipment you may need.

The second section in this chapter contains activities you can do to get your group or team started. As part of your preparation, it is important to review the principles of how adults learn so you can provide the proper environment in which your group or team will have a successful experience.

When a group or team first gets together, a facilitator must plan how the members will become acquainted and be ready to work as a team. Structured warm-up activities help participants get involved more quickly, increase their energy and interest, and help them to get to know each other as individuals. This chapter contains some examples of warm-up activities that you can use.

The last part of this chapter shows you how to set guidelines that will be the norm and agree upon expectations for the group or team to follow together. Since everyone will be having an opportunity to give feedback, the guidelines for giving feedback are also included.

COORDINATING THE ARRANGEMENTS

There are important details to take care of when facilitating a group or team, beyond thinking about their membership, roles and group process.

These are the administrative details that ensure finding an appropriate place to meet, having supplies on hand, printing, even parking permits. Think about what would happen if you forgot to obtain a flipchart and your plans called for one. Or what if you forgot to make arrangements for some beverages for the break?

The following checklist includes those administrative tasks most commonly done before, during and after a group meeting so that nothing is forgotten and everything gets done on time.

Following this master checklist are several other useful ones including one on selecting a meeting site and then evaluating the possible meeting room. Next, there's some information on five ways to set up a room. Finally, there is a supply and equipment checklist so you won't forget anything.

Review all of these checklists and modify them so that they include the items that pertain to your needs.

CHECKLIST OF ADMINISTRATIVE TASKS

Before the Meeting

- ______ Clarify your purpose for this new group or team
- ______ Identify a co-facilitator (if needed)
- ______ Identify potential group members
- ______ Review choices for meeting sites
- ______ Select date and time for first meeting
- ______ Draft agenda or design for first meeting
- ______ Identify and invite resource people
- ______ Finalize the site, date and time
- ______ Notify group members of meeting
- ______ Finalize agenda or meeting design
- ______ Prepare any materials for the meeting
- ______ Arrange for signs (if needed)
- ______ Arrange for visual aids
- ______ Order supplies and equipment
- ______ Confirm site arrangements
- ______ Arrange for food and beverages
- ______ Follow up with co-facilitator and resource people on all arrangements, materials, and introductions
- ______ Prepare agenda and evaluation form
- ______ Check on equipment and supplies
- ______ Complete all design details
- ______ Organize resource materials
- ______ Write introduction(s)
- ______ Arrange for transportation and parking permits
- ______ Prepare list of group members
- ______ Supervise delivery of equipment, supplies, and materials

Day of the Meeting

______ Inspect room for correct setup, temperature, and lighting
______ Put up signs
______ Double-check equipment and supplies
______ Give final meal count
______ Take care of any problems with food, beverages, room, equipment

During the Meeting

______ Check members' names for accuracy on list
______ Distribute and collect evaluations
______ Collect any bills

After the Meeting

______ Supervise return of equipment, supplies, and resource materials
______ Arrange for payment of bills
______ Tabulate evaluation forms
______ Send thank-you letter to resource people and others who helped

CHECKLIST FOR SELECTING A SITE

As you are looking at potential sites to hold your meetings, use the following list of criteria to evaluate each one:

______ **Proximity:** How close is this site to the largest number of group members?

______ **Cost:** Is there a charge for using this site?

______ **Flexibility:** Are there extra rooms nearby if we need them?

______ **People with Disabilities:** Is the site accessible to them?

______ **Beverages and Meals:** Can they be provided on site, in the room or nearby?

______ **Parking:** Is parking convenient? Is there a fee or permit?

______ **Smoking:** What is the policy on smoking?

______ **Equipment:** Does this site have equipment on hand? Is it free or is there a fee?

______ **Experience:** If you used this site before, was the experience good or bad? If bad, can those earlier problems be overcome?

CHECKLIST FOR EVALUATING A MEETING ROOM

As you are looking at potential meeting rooms, use this list of questions to help you consider each one:

______ **Atmosphere:** Is the room cheerful in colour and does it have outside windows?

______ **Layout:** Is the room large enough for your needs?

______ **Furniture:** Are the chairs comfortable for long meetings? Is the furniture movable?

______ **Conveniences:** How far away are the cloakrooms, fire exits, smoking area, lunchroom, lifts, food?

______ **Lighting:** Is there sufficient lighting? Can the room be darkened easily?

______ **Noise:** Is the room free of excessive noise and interruptions?

______ **Power points:** Are they available for your equipment?

______ **Heating:** Will the temperature be appropriate and can you control it yourself?

______ **Telephone:** Is there one nearby for participants to use privately? Is there one in the room – and, if so, do you want one there?

FIVE WAYS TO ARRANGE A ROOM

Assuming that your team consists of no more than eight people, there are several choices for setting up the room for optimal communications.

Circle: For an informal atmosphere, arrange the chairs in a circle with no tables.

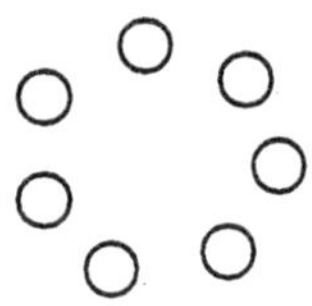

Semicircle: Place a flipchart on an easel in the open end of the semicircle.

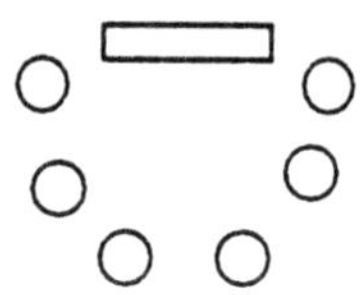

Round Table: If there will be a lot of writing, use a large round table. It is more difficult to use either a whiteboard or flipchart unless a space is left open at the table for you and this equipment.

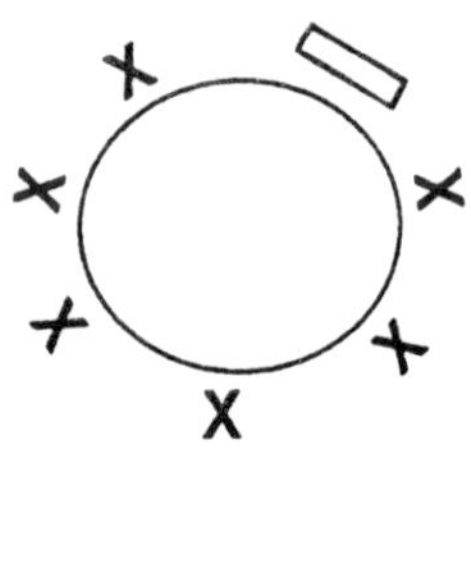

U-Shape: Form tables in a U-shape with chairs only on the outside. The open part of the U is for a flipchart. This information allows for writing, but people will have to crane their necks to see the others in their own row of chairs.

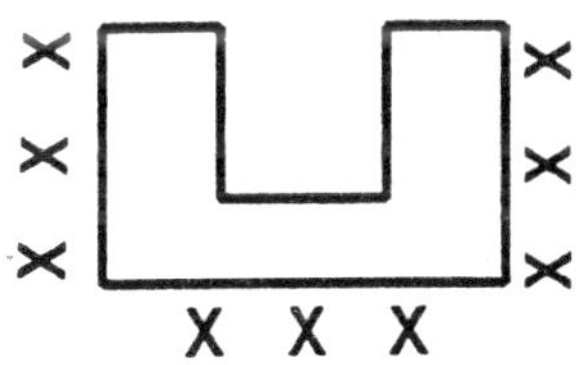

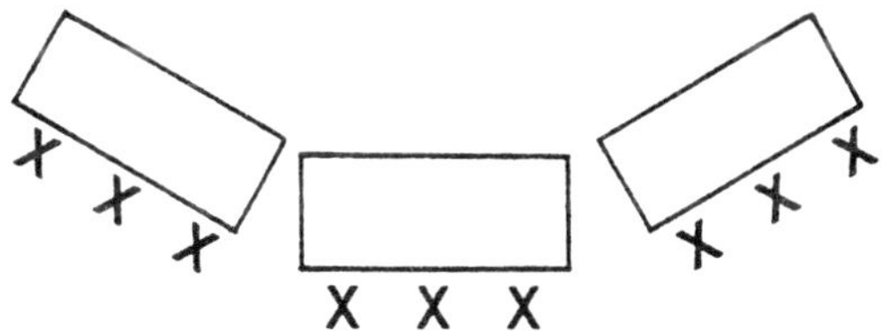

Herringbone: Arrange two sets of tables in a herringbone shape with chairs on the outside only. The facilitator and any equipment can face these two tables. This shape allows good eye contact among everyone.

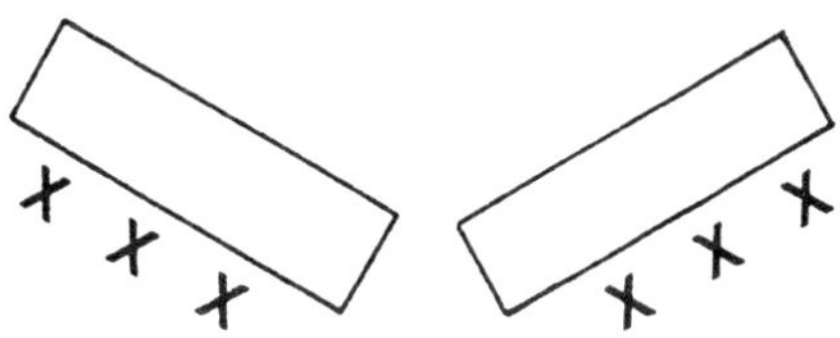

SUPPLY CHECKLIST

- ______ Acetate sheets
- ______ Blank paper
- ______ Flipchart pads
- ______ Folders
- ______ Magic markers
- ______ Masking tape
- ______ Name tags
- ______ Pencils
- ______ Pens
- ______ Scissors
- ______ Transparency pens
- ______ Whiteboard markers

EQUIPMENT CHECKLIST

- ______ Easels
- ______ Extension cords and adapter
- ______ Extra bulbs for projectors
- ______ Overhead projector
- ______ Screen
- ______ Tape recorder
- ______ Video player
- ______ Whiteboard

WARMING UP YOUR GROUP

Getting your team or group off on the right foot is an essential part of facilitation. Just going around and giving one's name and title is not sufficient.

Structured warm-up activities help participants to get involved more quickly, to increase their energy and interest, and to help them to get more acquainted with each other.

Some activities work best when the group first forms. Others can be used periodically to add more depth to the interpersonal relationships and variety to your process.

The following activities are just a few selected from *Saying Hello: Getting Your Group Started.* They meet three objectives:

1. To help clarify group members' expectations and knowledge.
2. To introduce them to working within a team.
3. To enhance the interpersonal relationships.

There are many more activities available from *Saying Hello: Getting Your Group Started, Icebreakers: A Sourcebook of Games, Exercises and Simulations* and others on the market. You might want to start a file of additional ideas so that you have a variety to choose from. Always adapt these activities to fit your objectives and group members' needs.

Sources of Activities:

Lois B Hart, *Saying Hello: Getting Your Group Started* (Leadership Dynamics, 875 Poplar Ave., Boulder, CO 80304, USA)

Ken Jones, *Icebreakers: A Sourcebook of Games, Exercises and Simulations* (Kogan Page, 120 Pentonville Road, London N1 9JN)

Some other training reference books will have sections devoted to warm-up activities.

Folding Arms

GOAL: To increase the members' receptivity to change

ESTIMATED TIME: 5–10 minutes

STEP 1: Introduce this activity by asking members to fold their arms in the manner that is their natural one. Observe the different positions people use to fold their arms such as both hands showing or tucked in, or which hand is placed on top of which arm.

STEP 2: Next ask the people to refold their arms in a different position and ask them how it feels. Keep them in this position so they see how it feels after a few minutes elapse.

STEP 3: Relate this folding arms activity to the purpose of this group or team. For instance, your group or team may be asked to address some difficult issues and seek some creative solutions and these may cause discomfort.

Suggest that they keep an open mind to change.

Around the Circle

GOAL: To give members the chance to share their expectations, goals, contributions or personal characteristics

ESTIMATED TIME: 5–10 minutes

STEP 1: Explain that we all have expectations when we join a new group or team. Give some examples.

STEP 2: Ask each person to silently think of one expectation that he/she has and would be willing to share.

STEP 3: Either in sequential or random order, ask each person to briefly state that expectation.

VARIATIONS: Use a different topic such as sharing:

'One goal I hope we achieve is . . .'

'One thing that will make it hard to achieve our goal is . . .'

'Something I can contribute to this group/team is . . .'

'I'm often called (Adjective + Name), for example "Organized Sam" or "Helpful Hannah".'

Where Would You Rather Be?

GOAL: To help members overcome a mental obstacle or distraction that would keep them from participating fully in this group or team experience.

ESTIMATED TIME: 10–15 minutes

STEP 1: Explain that we often wish we were somewhere else rather than participating in a new group or team. For example, often we are thinking about all the work left on our desk or what a great weekend we had!

STEP 2: Ask participants to get comfortable and close their eyes.

Slowly give these directions:

'Go to a place that gives you great pleasure. Look around you and take it all in. What are you seeing? How do you feel?

Choose something from this place, a thing, person or even a feeling, that you could bring back with you.

When you are ready, open your eyes.'

STEP 3: Ask for volunteers to share what they brought back.

COMMENT: This activity usually helps members relax and focus on their group or team's task so that you can get back to the business at hand.

SETTING GUIDELINES

When the team first meets, the members need to establish some guidelines for working together. Before that meeting, look over the following suggested guidelines. Modify and add more as needed. Prepare a list to distribute.

Next, explain why your team must agree on some guidelines. Agreement is a signal that everyone is committed to the team's efforts. Also, guidelines keep some conflicts from developing. Because you can refer to these guidelines they help to resolve problems that will emerge.

Distribute these guidelines and discuss each one until there is consensus. Write up a final list of guidelines and have each team member sign the agreement. Periodically review them; add and modify them as needed.

- We will be as open as possible but will honour the right of privacy.
- Information discussed in our group will remain confidential.
- We will respect differences. We won't discount others' ideas.
- We will be supportive rather than judgmental.
- We will give feedback directly and openly; it will be given in a timely fashion, and we will provide information that is specific and focuses on the task and process and not on personalities.
- Within our group, we have the resources we need to solve any problem that arises. This means that we will all be contributors.
- We are each responsible for what we get from this team experience. We will ask for what we need from our facilitator and the other group members.
- We will try to get better acquainted with each other so we can identify ways we can develop professionally.
- We will use our time wisely, starting on time, returning from breaks and ending our meetings promptly.
- When members miss a meeting we will share the responsibility for bringing them up to date.

- We will keep our focus on our goals, avoiding sidetracking, personality conflicts and hidden agendas. We will acknowledge problems and deal with them.
- We will not make phone calls or interrupt the group.

TEAM SIGNATURES

______________________	______________________
______________________	______________________
______________________	______________________
______________________	______________________

GUIDELINES FOR GIVING FEEDBACK

There are many opportunities for the facilitator and team members to give and receive feedback. As the facilitator, you must stay aware of what is happening. When you observe some behaviour that is either helpful or hindering, your role is to give feedback to that person.

As the process observer, you objectively listen and watch, then give feedback based on your observations. As a member of the team, it is also appropriate to share observations about the facilitator and the other team members.

The facilitator needs to create the environment where giving, receiving and asking for feedback is acceptable and beneficial. Set an example by giving feedback, which follows these guidelines. Distribute the guidelines so that group members and process observers follow them.

1. Be clear as to your **REASON** for giving feedback. Ask yourself why you are giving this feedback so that you are sure it will help the person receiving it.
2. Determine the **BEST TIME** to give the feedback. Generally it is best to give feedback immediately so your mind is fresh with your observation and the receiver will also recall the behaviour or incident. Sometimes it is better to delay giving feedback. For instance, you might need to wait until you see additional evidence of a behaviour. Or, the receiver might be very tired or distracted and a short delay might be needed so he/she will be more receptive.
3. **PLAN** what you'll say. To give objective feedback, refer to the process observation forms for ideas. When giving feedback to a person who is sensitive or creates problems, plan carefully what you'll say – and do it privately.
4. **LIMIT** negative feedback to behaviours that you think the receiver will be willing and able to change.
5. Give feedback **DIRECTLY**. People need to hear direct feedback on their behaviour; however, you need to consider if the feedback is best given in front of others or privately. Feedback on helpful behaviour will let the team know what is appreciated.

6. **DESCRIBE** behaviour rather than making judgments. Focus the feedback on the process you have observed and not on personalities.
7. **GIVE EXAMPLES** or specifics so the receiver can comprehend the information more completely.

The team can agree that they will do the following when they receive feedback:

- Look at the person giving the feedback.
- Ask for specifics and examples if they are not provided.
- Paraphrase to make sure the feedback was understood.

BUILDING AN AGENDA

An agenda is the road map for what the group or team wants to accomplish during a specified period of time. An agenda is valuable because it:

- Clarifies which tasks or issues need to be discussed
- Helps put these items into a ranked order
- Gives the facilitator an idea of how much time might be needed
- Provides the guidelines for measuring accomplishments
- Becomes the outline for developing a status report or group memory

Pre-Meeting Diagnosis

Many facilitators develop an agenda before the scheduled meeting. This ensures that sufficient information is identified about the group members and the issues that need to be addressed. These most important topics are then covered on the agenda.

If you are facilitating a meeting for the first time with a particular group or team, plan to meet the manager or leader in addition to representatives from the group.

If you are preparing an agenda for an ongoing group or team which you normally facilitate, you'll know the answers to the first three sections; but before each meeting, you will need to think about the questions in section 4. (Since the skill in asking questions is so important during these interviews, review the guidelines on asking questions found in Chapter 5.)

1. **Name of group or team and primary contact person:**

2. **Information on the members:**

   Who are they?

   What role does each play in this organization? Ask for a copy of the organizational chart.

   How well do they know each other?

   How many people will be attending?

3. **History of the group or team:**

   Why was this group or team formed?

   When was it formed?

   Does it have a written mission or vision statement? As for a copy.

   Which stage of group development are they in? (Refer to Chapter 2.)

   Describe the quality of the interpersonal relationships.

   What problem solving and decision making methods do they use?

4. **Roles:**

   Who decided that this group or team needed a facilitator?

   Do they have previous experience using a facilitator?

   Do they know that there will be a facilitator?

   Does anyone have experience as a recorder or process observer?

5. **Goals, Tasks and Issues:**

   What is the primary goal of this particular meeting?

   What tasks need to be accomplished in this meeting?

   What issues need discussion and resolution? Have they discussed them before?

   Will the appropriate decision-maker be present to finalize decisions?

6. **Administrative Details:**

   Where will the meeting be held? What kind of room/furniture does it have?

   What are the start and finish times?

   Have arrangements been made for food and beverages?

   Confirm the room setup and equipment/supply needs.

Preparing an Agenda

Prepare a preliminary agenda. Be sure to schedule time for a warm-up activity, breaks after every hour or hour and a half, meals, and closure activities. Groups are usually able to tackle a more difficult problem or task after some initial warm-up period and announcements.

Post the agenda or at least review it with the group or team. Explain the process that will be used and roles that will be played. Allow for members to ask questions and make suggestions for other items to be added.

Sometimes, facilitators wait until the group convenes to develop an agenda either because they have not had time to meet those who could help name the issues and tasks or because they want the members to take more ownership for the meeting. If you wait to develop an agenda, use the questions in section 3, 4, and 5. Use a flipchart to list potential items. Then discuss them until an order of items is agreed upon.

Using the Agenda

Stick to the agenda as best you can. Periodically, review what you think has been accomplished and preview what items are left. Make adjustments as needed but use group consensus. Be sure to keep to the announced times for breaks, meals and adjournment.

Often, too many items are placed on an agenda, so don't be surprised if everything isn't covered. Summarize those items that weren't covered and decide with the group if they could be accomplished by an individual or a subgroup or held until the next meeting. Make a record of this decision so that either individuals or subgroups can give reports at the next meeting. Also note the items that will be incorporated into the next agenda.

Finally, use the agenda as the outline for preparing a group memory or status report.

CREATING A GROUP OR TEAM VISION STATEMENT

Most groups that want to become functioning teams eventually will need to develop a statement of their vision. Groups without a vision never become a team; thus a group which wants to be a team needs to develop this statement early in its life.

What Is a Vision Statement?

Often the word *vision* is used synonymously with the word *mission*. In this book, the word *vision* will be used because it involves the process of visualizing something that is not actually seen or in existence yet. The word *mission* denotes religious and diplomatic functions, and is more limiting.

The development of a vision relies on the ability of the group or team members to imagine what they want and to describe their hopes and dreams. The process can be hard because it requires making the elusive more concrete. This requires using a collaborative process for reaching consensus.

A vision statement incorporates the individuals' wishes with the needs of the organization. The vision statement then becomes the blueprint and driving force for the group and for the team's existence.

Writing a Vision Statement

If you are responsible for helping a group develop its written vision statement, first review any organizational literature that is available because it will contain clues for writing a vision. Bring this literature to the meeting.

Start out with a definition of a vision as found in the dictionary:

> *'... the ability to perceive something not actually visible, as through mental acuteness or keen foresight'.*

Solicit members' reactions to this definition and their interpretation of the word 'mission' because many will be used to using mission instead of vision. Agree on which term they will use.

Next it is helpful for each person to reflect silently and then write out what they think the main purpose, goal, mission or vision is for their organization (or specific team).

Solicit and list each statement on the flipchart. The contributor can give a fuller explanation. Other members might want to ask questions for clarification.

If appropriate, distribute any organizational literature or written instructions given to this team. Have members discuss any variable that would affect the shaping of their vision.

Use consensus for making a decision on the vision. (See guidelines in Chapter 6.) This process takes time, so don't rush it.

The goal is to write a short statement of the vision, usually in one sentence. With a concise vision statement, individuals should be able to remember their vision easily.

For example, this vision statement incorporated both the *what* and *how*:

> *'We are a human resource team committed to our clients' success through training, organization development, consultation and publications.'*

Some vision statements consist of two parts, a short preamble of what they want to happen followed by how they will achieve the vision. For example, the preamble of what this agency wants to do might read:

> *'The Centre will specialize in the prevention of the misuse and abuse of alcohol and drugs.'*

Then the secondary statement tells how they will do it, so it might read:

> *'We will stimulate and mobilize local and national partnerships and facilitate the application of research and training methods to support the*

adoption and long-term success of community prevention and intervention programmes.'

Active verbs make a vision statement come alive, so help the group members edit their statement and add words that encourage action:

resolves	manages	provides
measures	coordinates	delivers
implements	administers	serves
tackles	creates	evaluates

Evaluating the Vision Statement

A well written vision statement stands the test of time and scrutiny. Post the statement in several prominent places so individuals continue to absorb its meaning and implication for their activities.

As the members explore solutions to problems, ask them to evaluate whether the proposed solution(s) are compatible with the vision.

Periodically review the vision, discuss its current usefulness, then adapt and rewrite it as needed.

Chapter 5

Mastering the Art of Facilitation

INTRODUCTION

The art of facilitation means using skills that can set you apart from other facilitators who know the mechanics of the role but lack some important people-skills. These include using interpersonal communication skills, developing the group's or team's working relationships, and judging your timing.

Although all communication skills are important in groups or teams, there are three that are crucial to facilitation. One is observation, the ability to see what is happening within the group or team and deciding how to respond. Listening and questioning skills are important, too, so that information is clarified before solutions are sought.

To develop the group's or team's working relationships, this chapter includes how to build commitment and synergy and also how to mediate conflicts between members.

Another facilitation skill is learning how to keep the energy flowing that will affect the productivity of the members. For variety, it helps to know how to regroup them too.

Many new facilitators have a difficult time judging how much time they need to allow for activities. Ways to develop this skill are covered at the end of this chapter.

WATCH FOR UNSPOKEN MESSAGES

The purpose in paying close attention to your group or team members is to observe what they are saying . . . or not saying.

About 50 per cent of all communication is conveyed non-verbally. As a facilitator, you need to watch for the unspoken messages that accompany what is said. As a process observer, you can also observe both messages.

Utilizing your observation skills can help you to assess the effectiveness of the group process and how well information is being received. Based on these observations, you can adjust your questions, introduce a new activity or procedure, call a break or deal with whatever is interfering with the success of the group.

Observations collected over time can help you to decide whether to continue the process being used or to modify it to respond better to their needs.

What Should You Be Looking For?

First, look at their faces, body positions, and how they move:

Is the person:

- smiling?
- frowning?
- nodding?
- yawning?
- looking at you or away?
- leaning forward or back in the chair?
- tapping a pencil or other item?
- shuffling their feet?

What Does It Mean?

Sometimes you can accurately guess what people are feeling based on what you are observing. For instance:

If they are:	*Then they may be feeling:*
Smiling Nodding affirmatively Leaning forward Maintaining eye contact	Enthusiasm and interest Agreement with what's happening
If they are:	*Then they may be feeling:*
Yawning Staring off into space Shuffling feet Leaning back in chair Looking at the clock	Boredom Fatigue Uninterested
If they are:	*Then they may be feeling:*
Frowning Scratching head Pursing lips Staring off into space Avoiding eye contact	Confusion Disagreement Suppression of feelings

Although a single behaviour can serve as an indicator of a feeling, accurate inferences will be based on all of the data you collect from observing your group members.

What Should You Do Next?

Whether you decide to take action or not will depend on the situation as you observe it. You need to assess how many group members are experiencing the observed feelings, the depth and possible duration of them, and their impact on the group's process and goals.

In your judgment, if the situation warrants action, consider the alternatives outlined here:

IF YOU HAVE OBSERVED	AND . . .	THEN . . .
Enthusiasm Interest Agreement	• Several group members display the behaviour,	• Continue, and make a mental note that the experience is well received.
	• One group member displays the behaviour,	• Involve this person more actively in the process.

IF YOU HAVE OBSERVED	AND . . .	THEN . . .
Boredom Fatigue Lack of interest	• Several group members display the behaviour,	• Take a break, • Speed up the process, • Review the group's goals, or • Introduce a new method or procedure.
	• One group member displays the behaviour,	• Talk with him/her privately.

IF YOU HAVE OBSERVED	AND ...	THEN ...
Confusion Disagreement	• Several group members display the behaviour,	• Ask them about areas of confusion, or • Give a new explanation.
Suppression of feelings	• One group member displays the behaviour,	• Ask this person about areas of confusion and provide clarification, or • Talk with the person privately.

SHOW YOU ARE PAYING ATTENTION

Facilitators must show they are paying attention. Group members quickly know if their facilitator is really there; they respond well when their facilitator makes the effort to pay attention to them.

You can show that you are paying attention to your group members in several non-verbal ways. By positioning yourself physically in a manner that shows that you are paying attention to them, you build rapport, communicate that you value them as individuals, and are interested in them.

This attending behaviour will help you to gather information about the members' needs and experiences. Your physical positioning enables you to observe their behaviours, which are important sources of information for you in assessing how the group activity is being received. It also encourages them to interact verbally with you.

Follow these guidelines as you facilitate and your group will know that you are paying attention:

DO	DON'T
• Position your body so you face all the group members.	• Turn your back to part of the group.
• Smile at individuals.	• Frown or look judgmental.
• Listen carefully while they talk.	• Shuffle papers or look at your watch while group members are talking.
• Keep eye contact.	• Avoid eye contact or stare at individuals.
• Nod affirmatively.	• Remain impassive.
• Talk with all group members.	• Talk to only a few people.
• Continually scan the group with your eyes.	• Scan too rapidly.

OBSERVING UNSPOKEN MESSAGES AND ATTENTIVENESS

Unspoken Messages:	How Facilitator Responded:
1. Smiling	
2. Frowning	
3. Nodding head	
4. Shaking head	
5. Looking away from speaker	
6. Looking at speaker	
7. Leaning back in chair	
8. Tapping pencil or feet	
9. Shuffling feet or papers	
10. Yawning	

HOW DID THE FACILITATOR SHOW HE/SHE WAS PAYING ATTENTION?

- Position of body: Faced entire team or turned back to some?
- Smiling or frowning: In response to what?
- Looking at speaker: Looked directly at them? Looked at watch or papers?
- Eye contact: Made with everyone or only some? Totally avoided it? Stared?
- Head movement: Nodded agreement? Shook head 'no'?
- Talked with: Everyone or only a few?

LEARN TO LISTEN

Listening is an essential skill used by effective facilitators. It requires hearing what someone says and also verifying that you heard and understood the information accurately.

The first step, listening to the words said, requires the facilitator's total concentration. The second step, paraphrasing, requires an accurate review of what was heard and verification that it was accurately understood. As a facilitator, learn and practise this skill. Also teach this skill to group members and anyone who is asked to serve as the recorder.

STEP 1: Listen carefully to the words being said.

As you listen to the words, look at the speaker and try to grasp both the content and the meaning of the words. While this may sound simple, you will find that the major roadblocks to listening to the speaker's words are the internal and external distractions that keep you from focusing on what they are saying.

Internal distractions are thoughts that develop inside you while someone else is talking. Sometimes they are related to what the person is saying. Sometimes you may be thinking about the next question you might ask. You must eliminate these internal distractions that keep you from focusing on what is being said.

External distractions are those things happening around you that compete with keeping your attention on the speaker. They can be noises outside the room, two people whispering or perhaps someone writing on a flipchart. Exclude them or, at least, defer giving attention to them until the person has finished speaking. Or stop the person speaking until this distraction is eliminated.

STEP 2: Paraphrase what was said:

Paraphrasing will clarify what the speaker said. Paraphrasing is not done all the time: it is especially helpful when the speaker rambles, giving conflicting or complex information, and a better understanding is necessary.

When paraphrasing, start with, 'I heard you saying . . .', or, 'As I understand it . . .' before paraphrasing what the speaker said. Ask the speaker if this was accurate. If it was, you can move on. If it was paraphrased inaccurately or important details were missed, the speaker can repeat the information needed to complete understanding.

ASKING QUESTIONS AND GETTING ANSWERS

Questions play a major role in facilitating groups. Questions invite participation and members' involvement. Questions get people to think about an issue from a different perspective. The facilitator asks questions to get feedback about how the group experience is working for the members.

There are three skills to learn and use as a facilitator:

1. Asking questions;
2. Handling the answers to your questions; and
3. Responding to questions directed to the facilitator.

1. Asking Questions

Asking questions effectively is one of the most important skills you'll need as a facilitator. This means selecting the right type of open-ended question, phrasing it so it elicits the response you are after and even directing the question appropriately.

There are two basic types of questions from which to choose: open-ended questions and closed questions. As you can see from this chart, it is better to learn how to ask the open-ended question because it elicits a more complete response and more participation.

Type of Question	Description	Example
Closed	• Requires a one-word answer • Closes off discussion • Usually begins with 'is', 'can', 'how many' or 'does'.	'Does everyone understand the changes we've discussed?'
Open-ended	• Requires more than a 'yes' or 'no' answer • Stimulates thinking • Elicits discussion • Usually begins with 'what', 'how', 'when', or 'why'.	'What ideas do you have for explaining the changes to our customers?'

The second step to asking an effective question is to determine how to phrase it so that the group members remain focused. The key to phrasing questions is to follow these guidelines:

DO	DON'T
• Ask clear, concise questions covering a single issue.	• Ask rambling, ambiguous questions covering multiple issues.
• Ask challenging questions which will provoke thought.	• Ask questions that don't provide an opportunity for thought.
• Ask reasonable questions based on what group members know.	• Ask questions that most of them can't answer.
• Ask honest and relevant questions.	• Ask 'trick' questions.

As a facilitator you also need to think about how to direct questions toward group members. There are two ways to direct questions: either to everyone in the group or to a specific person. Follow these guidelines so that you direct questions appropriately.

IF YOU WANT TO . . .	THEN . . .
Stimulate everyone's thinking.	Direct the question to the group.
Allow them to respond voluntarily or avoid putting an individual on the spot.	Ask a question such as: 'What experiences have any of you had with this problem?'
Stimulate one person to think and respond.	Direct the question to that individual.
Tap the known resources of an 'expert' in the group.	Direct the question thus: 'Mary, you have had a lot of experience in applying these regulations with customers. What would you do in this case?'

2. Handling Answers to Questions

The second skill associated with the questioning process involves the way in which you handle group members' answers to your questions.

This will not only impact on the individual who gave the answer but will also affect the amount of future participation you will receive from the other group members.

In the following examples, you will see how three guidelines are used:

1. Always reinforce correct answers positively.
2. Acknowledge the effort of the respondent, regardless of the answer given.
3. Minimize potential embarrassment for wrong or incomplete answers.

If the answer is correct, then use positive reinforcement such as, 'Yes, that's right,' or, 'What a useful observation!'

If the answer is partially incorrect, reinforce the part that is correct, then repeat the question or redirect it to someone else. For example, 'You are on the right track. What other ideas do you have?' or, 'That's a good point. Who else has some alternatives?'

If the answer is incorrect, acknowledge the effort, then redirect the question to others in the group. For instance, 'I can see how you might come up with that. Who else has an idea?'

3. Responding To Questions

As the facilitator, you will also be asked questions, so you need to know how to respond to them. When this happens you have three choices:

1. Provide the answer yourself when you are the only person who can do so.
2. Redirect the question when there is a high probability that the same person or someone else will be able to come up with the correct answer.
3. Defer the question when it is beyond the scope of the group or you need time to find out the correct answer.

OBSERVING QUESTIONING SKILLS

When the facilitator asked questions, what words did they begin with? Were they open-ended or closed questions? Were they directed at the team or individuals?

	Beginning Word	Open/Closed	Directed at Team/Individual
1.			
2.			
3.			
4.			
5.			
6.			
7.			
8.			
9.			
10.			

When team members answered the questions asked by the facilitator, give examples of how the facilitator:

1. Reinforced correct answers positively;
2. Acknowledged the effort of the respondent, regardless of answer given; and
3. Minimized potential embarrassment for wrong or incomplete answers.

BUILDING COMMITMENT AND SYNERGY

As a facilitator, you will need to know how to develop your team's interpersonal relationships. You laid the groundwork for establishing interpersonal commitment with the team's guidelines, but you also need to provide additional activities that will reaffirm their commitment and synergy.

Synergy is the outcome of the team members' hard work as they clarify their goals, identify their responsibilities, and work on their development. Synergistic teams respect one another and feel a special bond. Teams just know when synergy is present.

Special activities can help the team members focus on what is helping or hindering their unity and trust, to identify behavioural patterns and roles, and to practise more appropriate ones. These activities should be interjected periodically to facilitate commitment and synergy.

The following are some examples of activities used to develop commitment and synergy. They are only briefly described here. You'll need to build a collection of ideas by talking with other facilitators and reviewing books on training and team development.

Self-Interest

State how people participate fully in a group or accept change only when they feel that their self-interest is met. On a flipchart, draw several small umbrellas held by stick people. Group members individually decide how they would benefit by participating in this group or by accepting a change. Each writes the benefit on one of the umbrellas.

Next, draw one large umbrella, representing the total group, over all the individual umbrellas. The group discusses how its individual self-interests fit under the common umbrella of the whole group's self-interest.

Team Symbol

Individuals identify and sketch an object that symbolizes them. The team then draws one team symbol that incorporates the individual symbols into one new one. They sign the symbol. Refer to the team symbol periodically.

The Sinking Ship

This activity is typical of those that are done outdoors. It requires the team to take risks while solving a physical problem. In this activity, a rock or other natural object is identified as a lifeboat. It must be smaller than the space needed for the whole team to stand on it together. The team is given 10 minutes to decide how everyone will fit into the boat and hold their position for one full minute.

Cooperative Games

Structured activities encourage group members to work together. In one game, 'Cooperative Squares', individual members are given different pieces of a puzzle that must be assembled with the silent cooperation of the other team members.

Trust Activities

One person stands in the middle of a circle surrounded by the other members. With eyes closed, this person literally falls and the team must be trusted to break the fall before this person hits the ground.

Problem Solving

When teams must solve a problem, whether real or simulated, they also demonstrate that the team is more productive working together than if individuals were working alone. Simulated survival problems such as 'Lost on the Moon' or 'Lost at Sea' require individuals to rank which items they would choose for their survival. Then the whole team ranks these items and their list is compared with the rankings provided by survival experts.

Building a Bridge

The team must build a bridge out of newspaper and tape that is strong enough to hold a brick. As the team works at solving this kind of problem, a process observer can note roles people play and how the team works together.

Sharing Positive Feedback

When synergy is present, team members readily and easily say what they appreciate about one another, give unsolicited supportive feedback on tasks and freely share their ideas and experiences. To achieve this goal, the facilitator often guides the sharing of positive feedback during and at the end of team meetings.

MEDIATING CONFLICT BETWEEN TWO PEOPLE

As a facilitator, you will need to improve interpersonal relationships by helping group members resolve conflicts between themselves. Unresolved conflicts will negatively affect the productivity of the group and the team members' relationships.

Most people do not like conflict and will want to avoid the uncomfortable feelings associated with it. Therefore, as their facilitator, you need to be confident in helping them to face these conflicts.

When there is a conflict between two people, you can serve as their mediator. The following process can be used with the whole team present. The value of demonstrating this process with the whole team is that they all learn how to be mediators and increase their skills at resolving conflicts. Resolve the conflict privately if that is the best solution.

STEP 1: Discuss with the group occasions when the presence of a third party can help in resolving a conflict. Give some examples. Suggest that this process is one that this team can use now and in the future to work through conflicts between two people. Get their commitment to proceed.

STEP 2: The two people in conflict sit facing each other. You sit so you can see their faces clearly.

STEP 3: Ask one person to explain what the conflict is about and how they feel. The second person first listens, then is asked to paraphrase what was said. Then the second person states what they think the problem is about and how they feel. The first person listens, then is asked to paraphrase what was said.

STEP 4: In the second round, the first person now states the desired outcome which the second person paraphrases. Then the second person states the desired outcome which is paraphrased by the first person.

STEP 5: This process of stating, listening and paraphrasing is continued. The goal is to clarify the issues, hear the desired outcomes and find a solution between the two people. When consensus is reached and both agree to a solution, the process is complete.

STEP 6: Together, evaluate how this mediation process worked. First, ask the two participants how it felt and what steps of the process helped. Then ask the other group members for their observations. Discuss how this mediated process could be used in the future.

For more activities you could use with your group or team, see titles in the '*Training Activities*' series, published by Kogan Page.

KEEPING THE ENERGY FLOWING

Energy does ebb and flow in group members and also in the facilitator! It is important to keep some energizing ideas handy so that energy can be sustained and thus productivity increased.

Here are four categories of ideas to use:

Vary What Happens, When and Where

Variety in activity and even location can help energy levels. No one can stay awake with the very same activity all of the time so prepare a sequence of activities and topics that provides variety. For instance, combine discussion of a serious issue with something lighter and even humorous. Or use part of a work session on solving a problem and another evaluating how the group is working together.

Regroup people regularly. If you form subgroups to work on a problem, be sure to vary the group once in a while. Use place cards to force people to sit with different people occasionally.

People's metabolism dictates when they will have the most energy so half of your group may be alert in the morning, a large number will come awake in the afternoon and a small number will wish you could meet in the evening. Vary the time when you meet so that you can draw upon the energy of the group members.

Also vary where you meet once in a while. By meeting in different locations of a large organization, people get to see where their colleagues work. Try occasionally meeting in a setting away from work. Variety provides a fresh perspective.

Energize With Exercise

Provide for some physical exercise to re-energize the group. When they seem tired, do some yawning and stretching together. Have a set of several easy exercises that can be done in your meeting room. Often there is someone in the group who would be glad to conduct these exercise breaks.

Schedule walks, even if it is only around the building. The whole group could walk together, or group people in pairs and give them something to talk about while they take a ten minute walk.

Breaks

There should be a break about every hour because that's about as long as people can sit still and concentrate. Breaks are needed for visits to the loo, a quick phone call, getting a breath of fresh air, networking, or a smoke, if permitted on the site.

Smokers need about seven minutes to complete their routine, so tell them that's exactly how much time they have!

Food and Beverages

Food and beverages can help a meeting; however, the wrong ones can hinder it. Many people drink too much coffee because that is all that is available and the excessive caffeine leaves them irritable and tense. So if there will be beverages, provide a variety: tea (including herbal), coffee, diet and regular soft drinks, juices, even mineral water and milk.

The same holds true with food. The traditional doughnut or Danish pastry has so much sugar that it leaves people with a quick high and then a drop in energy. Select breads or muffins with less sugar, add juice or fruit and you'll find them sustaining their energy longer.

This is also true of snacks; keep a bowl of fruit or 'energy' bars available so that those who need food can get it easily. If you all eat lunch together, try to pick a lighter menu, or at least take time for a walk after the meal.

GROUPING AND REGROUPING

As you work for longer periods of time with your team, there will be a need to regroup team members. Grouping members creatively and periodically increases participation and adds variety to the experience.

Initially you may want to pair people so they can get better acquainted. You may want to form groups of three to brainstorm solutions that will then be shared with the total group. Or you may form groups of various sizes to discuss their common experiences with a particular issue.

Use your observation skills to determine when it is time to regroup people. For instance, if you notice interest and energy lagging, regroup them into small groups to work on a task. This will force more participation.

If you notice that a few people are consistently withdrawn, group the quieter ones together so the talkers can't dominate.

If you are concerned because different points of view are not being accepted, regroup people first by similar then later by dissimilar views.

Trust your instincts when you think it is time for the group to make a change. Also use your instincts to determine the formation of some of these subgroups. For example, if you are trying to pair the group members, ask yourself, 'Who would benefit from being with each other?'

Here are some of the more common ways to regroup people:

- ***Shared Views*** – Group people who hold similar views; then regroup them so that different views are represented.
- ***Roles*** – Group people based on similar roles; or vary them based on the different levels of work in their organization or mix them up so each department is represented.
- ***Years in Work or Profession*** – In each group, have a variety of experience represented in the work force, a particular profession or business.

If you periodically need to mix your total group, here are some suggestions on how to regroup them quickly and creatively:

- ***By Gender*** – Group by same gender or mixed gender.
- ***Birth Month*** – Group people born in same month or time of year.
- ***Birth Order*** – Group those who were 'only children', those who were firstborn, those who were 'middle children' and those who were born last.
- ***Shoe Sizes*** – Put those with large feet in one group.
- ***Hair or Eye Colours*** – Mix or match by colour of hair or eyes.
- ***Food Preference*** – Group people by their preference for Italian, Chinese, or Indian foods.
- ***Origin of Birth*** – Mix people up by where they were born, including different regions of the country or different parts of the world.
- ***By Metabolism*** – In a trio, try to have someone whose energy is high in the morning, another who is best in the afternoon and a third who works best in the evening.

TACKLING YOUR TIMING

Inexperienced facilitators often ask, 'How much time should I allow for doing a group activity?' or, 'When do I know if the group has taken enough time to discuss a topic fully?' As you'd expect, one's judgment on timing improves with experience. However, facilitators never seem to be perfect at predicting the amount of time needed.

Judging your timing is very intuitive. Decide from the moment you start to facilitate a group that you will listen to your gut feelings to determine the answer to your questions on timing.

Timing requires patience, so decide to be patient with the group and its process. You may know where you want them to go and how they might get there, but you need to guide them patiently in that direction. If you rush them, they may not fully explore an issue or learn how to resolve their problems.

Trust your instinct. Usually your first impression or reaction is right, so if it says, 'Seek closure', listen and act.

If you're using one of the problem solving or decision-making methods outlined in this book, suggested time lines are given. If you've selected an activity that doesn't have a time line, calculate how much time you think each part might take, then add about 25 per cent more. If you are still unsure, ask another facilitator whether they think you've calculated accurately.

Do a dress rehearsal of the activity to help you test the amount of time it might take participants to read directions and do what is asked of them. If you are doing an important activity with the group and they are working well on it, don't rush them. Instead, be flexible about the remainder of your plans with them. Be ready to trim or drop certain components of your design. It is better to trim your plans than to rush them too much.

Ask the group how the timing is for them. They'll let you know if it is too fast, too slow or just right.

When the timing feels right, grab the opportunity. Sometimes, ideas that were ruled out earlier may now be accepted. When desperation and frustration peak, it is often the best time for you to suggest a solution that incorporates the best of all the ideas offered. The members probably realize they are stuck and may welcome your consensus-testing.

If the group cannot finish within the amount of time available in that particular session, review what they have accomplished and identify any work they can do between sessions to work on the problem. At the beginning of the next session, review what they have done and suggest any changes in methods or activities they used.

Chapter 6

Tackling Problems and Making Decisions

INTRODUCTION

Once you have laid groundwork with your group or team, they will be ready to tackle the problems that they have identified.

This chapter includes several problem solving and decision-making methods that you can introduce to your group or team.

They include the Nominal Group Technique which helps to clarify a problem; the Fishbone, to identify causes and effects; three methods for collecting data about a problem; Brainstorming, which helps to unleash alternative solutions; and Force Field Analysis, which identifies those forces that work for and against proposed solutions.

Collaborating to reach consensus is commonly used in many groups and teams as a primary decision-making tool. However, many people misunderstand the purpose and use of consensus. Therefore, a description and guidelines are included in this chapter.

After you try any of these methods, evaluate their effectiveness with the form found on page 107.

THE NOMINAL GROUP TECHNIQUE TO CLARIFY AND RANK PROBLEMS

The nominal group technique is used after a list of problems is identified and you want to clarify the issues.

This is a very structured process that involves full participation by all the group members. This non-threatening method provides anonymity for individuals and yet ensures a broad based collection of opinion on defined problems.

You will need a recorder and two flipcharts to help you get all the issues clarified. Participants usually feel a real sense of accomplishment and commitment to future action after using the nominal group technique.

STEP 1: Silent Generation of Ideas

The group decides on a problem they want to clarify. Write the problem statement on the flipchart and also have group members write it on a sheet of paper.

Each person silently thinks about the problem then writes his/her thoughts relating to the problem on paper. These are usually short written phrases which focus on the problem and not solutions.

Everyone must be silent during this step.

STEP 2: Round Robin Reporting of Ideas

Next begin the round robin reporting of ideas using individuals' notes made in Step 1. Starting with a volunteer ask for one idea, which is recorded on the flipchart. Next ask who else has a similar idea and add this to the flipchart.

Using this process, continue to ask each person to contribute one idea until everyone has made a contribution. If they want to, a person can choose to pass in this first round, but eventually everyone is encouraged to make some contribution.

The round robin collection of ideas and recording them on the flipchart continues as long as people have new ideas to contribute.

No discussion of the ideas is done in this step.

When all of the ideas are recorded, label each one with a letter of the alphabet which will help in Step 4.

STEP 3: Discussion for Clarification

Now open up the discussion for the purpose of clarifying any of the ideas that were contributed. Group members are encouraged to ask each other the meaning of words and phrases that were recorded on the flipchart.

The purpose of this step is to provide individuals with the opportunity to give fuller explanations of their ideas. Make sure that ideas are not evaluated and do not allow arguments to develop.

STEP 4: Ranking of Problems

Give each group member five 3″ × 5″ cards. Looking over the ideas on the flipchart, each person selects the five items that, to them, have the highest priority. They either write the code letter or the idea on the card, with one selection per card. This should be done silently.

When this is completed, each person is asked to rank their five cards in the order of importance to them. The number 5 is the item of greatest importance with the number 1 the least important. Be sure they number their cards in this way because it is the opposite of what they would ordinarily do.

All the cards are collected and the rankings are tallied on a master sheet on the flipchart. The item with the largest number is ranked as the most important for the group to address.

After these four steps are completed, the group will be ready to use the other decision-making and planning tools found in this book.

How Much Time Should This Take?

The introduction of this method and explanation of the steps takes about 5 minutes. Allow 5–10 minutes for the silent generation of ideas. The recording of individuals' ideas will depend on the number that had been generated but, if discussion is avoided, all ideas should be recorded within half an hour. The discussion can be limited or allowed to go on indefinitely, but permit a minimum of twice the amount of time you used in Step 2. If it took 30 minutes to record the ideas, facilitate the discussion for up to 1 hour. The ranking and tallying of the results could take another 10–20 minutes.

IDENTIFYING CAUSES WITH THE FISHBONE

The method commonly called the Fishbone helps you to identify the probable causes behind a stated problem, or effect. The advantage of this method is that it presents a graphic representation of all the causes of a problem, irrespective of number.

The shape of the diagram looks like a fishbone, which explains how it got this name. It was originally developed by Dr. Kaoru Ishikawa, so sometimes it is called the 'Ishikawa'.

An Effect (or Problem)

Initially, you will need to help the team understand the difference between an effect and its causes. An effect is a quality problem or defect. An effect is usually the result of various causes. You may want to substitute the word 'problem' for effect.

For example, in a manufacturing setting, an effect could be that too many defective items are returned by consumers. In a service organization, an effect might be that there are too many customer complaints.

The Causes

The second part of this method identifies what causes the effect (or problem) to occur. These causes could be an:

Action	Activity	Attitude	Behaviour
Force	Policy	Procedure	Process

The cause could be because one of the above either exists or doesn't exist. For example, the lack of a policy can be a cause as much as a poorly written one can be.

Some people who use this method suggest that there are four general categories of causes:

Manpower　　Machines　　Methods　　Materials

These four categories may accurately describe the causes of problems in your organizational setting. However, you might want to change the name of these categories to describe your situation more accurately. You may also want to think of other major categories that causes might fall into. Examples might include:

Customers　　Environment　　Personnel　　Policies　　Procedures

Identifying the categories before listing causes might encourage team members to think of more types of causes. On the other hand, you might find that this arbitrary listing of categories inhibits creativity.

Guidelines for Using the Fishbone

STEP 1: Select an effect (or problem):

Often you will be given a problem for your team to work on or will already have chosen a critical one that needs immediate attention. However, if this has not occurred, ask the members to name some problems that are important to them and list them on the flipchart. Be sure they do not try to find solutions because at this point you are only trying to identify possible problems to solve.

Next, discuss the list of possible problems sufficiently so they can reach agreement on which one is the most critical to work on first.

Clarify the problem until everyone understands it.

STEP 2: Draw a diagram like this on a flipchart and write the effect/problem statement on the right of the horizontal line and arrow.

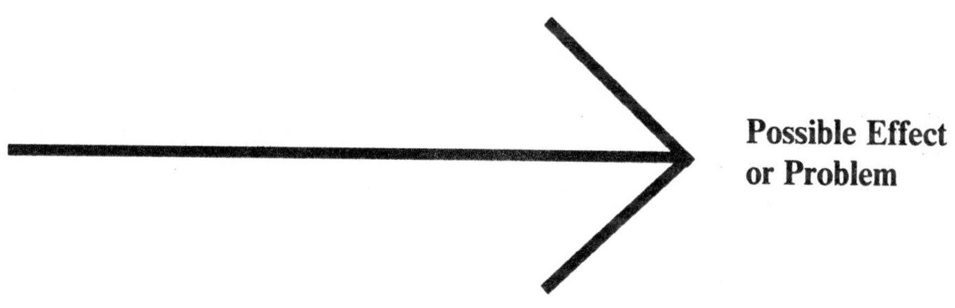

STEP 3: The team next identifies the major causes of the effect/problem. Each cause is listed separately on a diagonal line off of the horizontal line. The diagram now looks like the skeleton of a fish. If you have pre-determined the categories

of causes, draw that number of diagonal lines from the main bone.

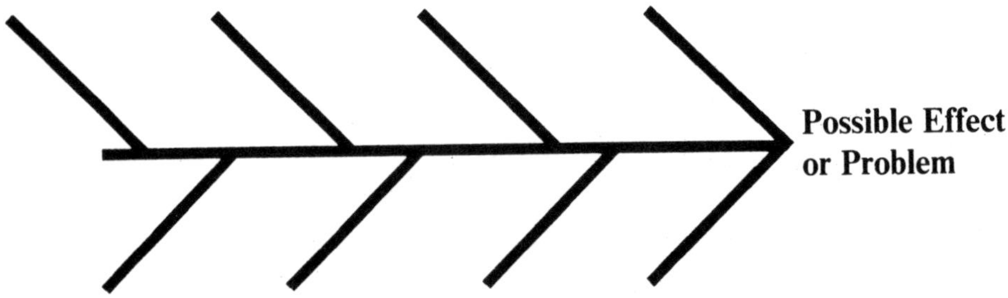

STEP 4: Next, details are added under each major category of a cause. Continue to have members address the reasons for the cause, and list them on the secondary diagonal lines. Even subparts can be drawn. With these added details drawn in, the diagram now has bones on the fish's skeleton:

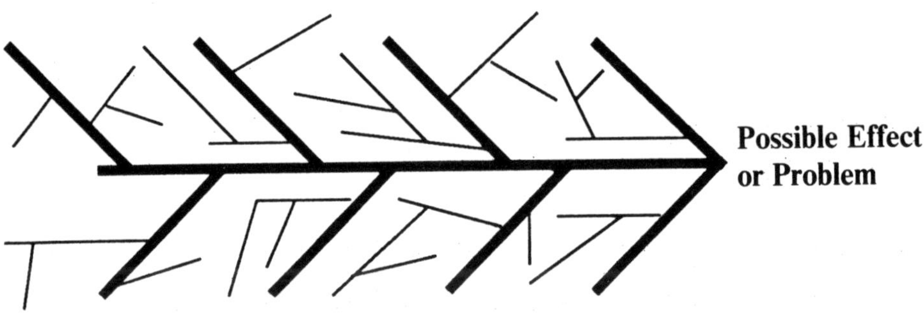

STEP 5: Once the list of causes is made, lead a discussion on them for the purpose of prioritizing the list. Put a number 1 by the greatest cause, a number 2 on the second greatest and so forth.

STEP 6: Follow-up by applying the Force Field Analysis to the primary cause and brainstorming to name possible solutions. (See guidelines on these methods in this chapter.)

COLLECTING DATA ABOUT A PROBLEM

When a group or team has identified a critical problem, they may need to collect some data about the problem and how often it happens. Methods for collecting data can help uncover additional information about a problem or issue and also verify their causes before solutions are sought.

There are three methods that you could use to gather this data.

1. Talk to people.
2. Do a survey or questionnaire.
3. Observe the problem as it happens.

1. Talk To People

a. Decide on the key questions that need to be asked and develop a form or format you will use to record the answers.
b. Determine if you will talk to individuals separately or in small focus groups.
c. Select a random sample of those who experience this problem.
d. Contact these people and set up the interviews.
e. Conduct the interviews using the selected form or format to record information.
f. Summarize the answers in an appropriate manner so that the team members can use this information for their next step in solving the problem.

2. Do a Survey or Questionnaire

a. Decide on the questions that will be asked and develop a survey or questionnaire.
b. Determine how you will distribute it.
c. Select a random sample of those who experience this problem.
d. Contact these people and send them the survey.
e. Collect the surveys and summarize the answers in an appropriate manner so that the team members can use this information for their next step in solving the problem.

3. Observe the Problem

The Checksheet is a very simple method of observing and tallying the problem every time it happens. For instance, in a manufacturing setting, the Checksheet is a simple matrix listing the errors in the left column with space to the right for recording it each time it occurs.

Name of Problem: ______			
Error	**Mark When it Occurs**	**Total**	**% of Total**

Another example is the concern of the team in a retail store about the problem of increasing numbers of returns. The first step they take is to determine the possible causes of the returns, which are listed in the left-hand column. Then they keep track for one day (or more) of every return made and tally the reasons.

Name of Problem:	Too Many Returns		
Possible Reason for Returns	**Mark When it Occurs**	**Total**	**% of Total**
Customer chose wrong size, colour	✓ ✓ ✓ ✓ ✓	5	25
Item was defective	✓ ✓ ✓	3	15
Item was a duplicate	✓ ✓	2	10
Customer changed his/her mind	✓ ✓ ✓	3	15
Customer found item at lower price elsewhere	✓ ✓ ✓ ✓ ✓ ✓ ✓	7	35
	Totals	20	100

This data revealed that the primary reason for returns was that the customers found the same item at another store for a lower price. Next, the store's team will consider alternatives to correct this problem.

BRAINSTORMING TO UNLEASH ALTERNATIVES

Successful problem solving depends on the group believing that solutions exist and creatively identifying all alternatives. Under a time restraint the brainstorming technique forces many ideas to emerge. The process is done in a non-judgmental atmosphere where all ideas are valued.

There are probably individuals in your group who have experienced the brainstorming technique. Since most people find this a useful and often enjoyable experience, their energy and enthusiasm will help to make this brainstorming session successful.

STEP 1: Introduce the purpose and steps of brainstorming. Select a recorder and set up the flipchart so everyone can see what will be recorded. Two recorders using flipcharts can help you gather ideas more quickly in Step 4.

STEP 2: Clarify which problem will be discussed. Write it on the flipchart.

STEP 3: Review the ground rules:

- Quantity, not quality: Use the time to think of as many solutions as possible. The more bizarre, the better.
- Piggyback: If someone else's idea triggers a slight variation of an idea for you, call it out.
- No evaluation: All ideas are accepted. No judgment of ideas is allowed at this time. Do not stop to discuss the *pros* and *cons* of any suggestion.
- Stop immediately at the end of five minutes.

STEP 4: Announce how much time will be used and immediately solicit solutions. The recorder writes as quickly as possible all of the ideas suggested, abbreviating in order to keep up with the group's suggestions. Stop when the time is up.

STEP 5: Review and evaluate alternatives. The group evaluates each suggestion according to the following criteria:

Impossible: Cross out those that are unrealistic or incompatible with your situation.

Maybe: put an 'M' next to those you might consider.
Outstanding: put an asterisk (*) next to those that strike you as especially creative, realistic, or appealing.

How Much Time Should This Take?

Take about 3–5 minutes to introduce brainstorming and get everything set up. Usually the actual brainstorming is limited to 5–15 minutes depending on the complexity of the problem. The evaluation step could take from 15–60 minutes depending on the depth of the discussion.

FORCE FIELD ANALYSIS TO IDENTIFY THE FORCES FOR AND AGAINST YOU

The Force Field Analysis technique is useful after a number of problems are identified, discussed and perhaps ranked. This tool tackles one problem at a time by analysing the forces that work against any change or potential solutions. It also identifies those forces that can help to bring about proposed changes and solutions.

STEP 1: Make copies of the Force Field Analysis form (page 103) and draw the same design on a flipchart. Even better, put two flipcharts side by side with one listing the Driving Forces and the other listing the Restraining Forces.

If several small groups do this activity simultaneously, each group can record the information on a copy of this handout.

STEP 2: List one of the group's top-ranking problems in the 'Problem' box. This represents the *current state of affairs*. The group needs to understand and agree upon the problem statement.

STEP 3: Next write a goal statement in the 'Goal' box. This should answer the question: 'What is the desired change?'

STEP 4: There are always numerous forces impacting on a desired change, some of which make the problem seem formidable and some of which encourage solutions to it. That is, there are forces that restrain change and also forces that facilitate change.

Make a list of each set of forces. Think of the current state of affairs as being held stationary by two sets of opposing forces.

First, list all the driving forces that would encourage the change to happen. The list of forces should include psychological, interpersonal, organizational, and societal factors.

STEP 5: Next, list all the restraining forces that prevent change from happening. Include all types of factors. If a force seems to be made up of multiple obstacles, each individual element should be listed separately.

Avoid arguing over the forces at this time. Suspend critical judgment and encourage understanding of each other's views. Create an accepting atmosphere.

STEP 6: Rank the restraining forces as to which are the strongest and thus most difficult to change. The goal is first to reduce those forces that have the least resistance or are the easiest to resolve.

Also rank the driving forces as to their strength. The goal is to capitalize on those that will get the greatest changes into motion first.

How Much Time Should This Take?

Allow about 5 minutes to introduce this technique and explain the steps. Assuming you facilitate the process, it should take about one hour to complete the other five steps. If small groups simultaneously complete the worksheet, allow an additional 15–30 minutes for those groups to report back to the total group.

Force Field Analysis

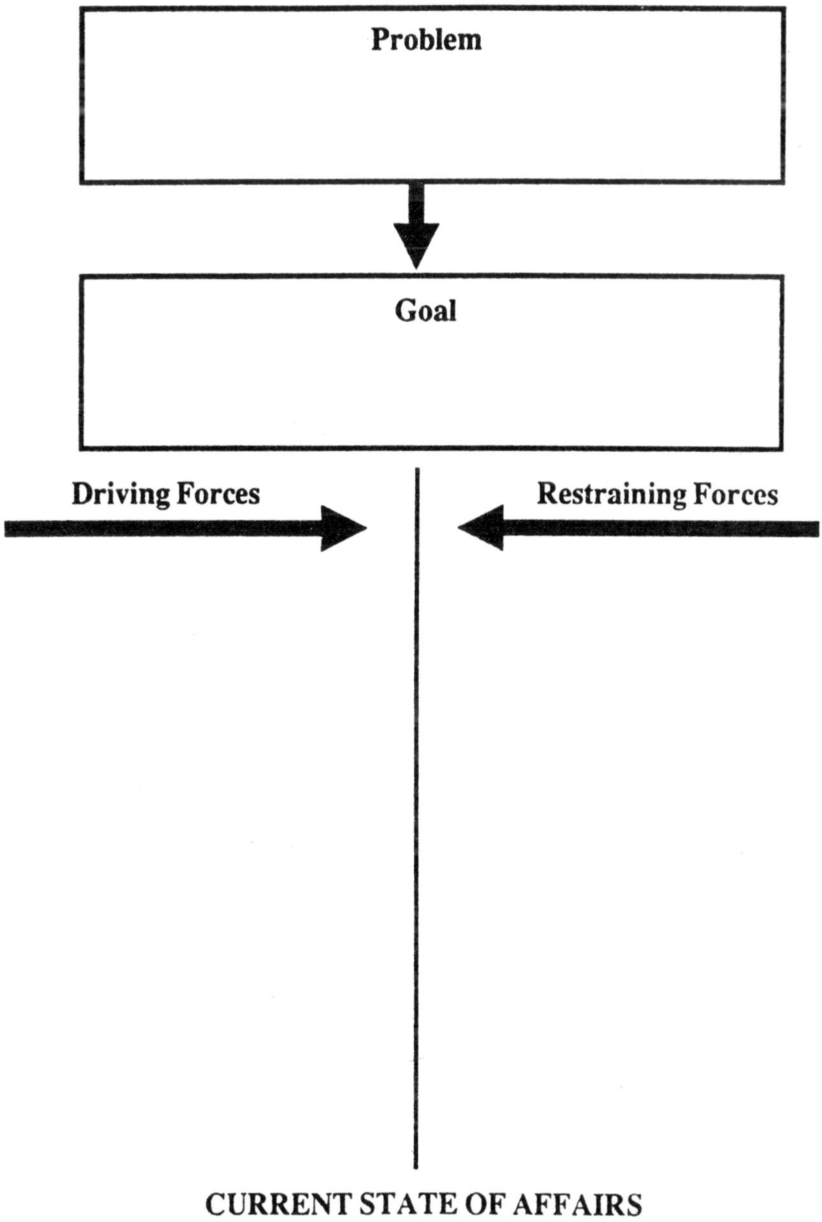

REACHING AGREEMENT WITH CONSENSUS

Groups often collaborate closely in order to reach consensus or agreement on a problem, solution, or action plan.

This consensus technique requires the recognition of, and respect for, every group member's ideas, opinions, and suggestions. Therefore, this tool works best after the group has shown a commitment to working together in a cooperative manner and has demonstrated mutual trust and respect toward one another.

Reaching consensus in a group is never easy; however, it can result in both high morale and successful accomplishment of tasks.

As the facilitator, you will first review the guidelines for reaching consensus (on page 105). Then you need to find out who has knowledge about, or experience with, the problem you are trying to solve. You will need to ask for this because individuals who could be a resource to the group or team generally will not volunteer this information. They fear being labelled a 'know-all' or dominator when, in fact, their knowledge and experience are essential to reaching consensus.

Consensus is usually reached after the group members talk at length, listen to each person's point of view, and explore their own knowledge. Therefore, reaching consensus takes a lot of time and must not be rushed.

Consensus requires each member of the group to agree on the point being discussed before it becomes a part of the group's decision. Not every point will meet with everyone's complete approval. Unanimity is not the goal, although you may reach it unintentionally. It is not necessary for every person to be satisfied, but at least all ideas are thoroughly reviewed.

The goal is to have individuals accept a point of view based on logic. When all group members can understand and accept the logic of a differing point of view, your group may assume that it has reached consensus. Of course, this also means a single person can block the group process.

GUIDELINES FOR REACHING CONSENSUS

Before starting the discussion, the following guidelines must be reviewed with the group. Keep copies handy so that any group member can remind the others if they lose their way in following them.

TO ACHIEVE CONSENSUS, WE WILL . . .

- Take time to learn what each of us knows that could help us to solve the problem.
- Avoid arguing over individual rankings or position. We each will present a position as lucidly and logically as possible, and will seriously consider what the other group members are presenting.
- Avoid 'win-lose' stalemates. When an impasse occurs, we will look for the next most acceptable alternative for both parties.
- Avoid changing our minds just to avoid conflict.
- Not vote or toss coins because these do not lead to consensus. We will treat differences of opinion as an indication that we have not shared enough information or explored our resources.
- Keep the attitude that different views are both natural and healthy to our group or team, rather than a hindrance.
- View initial or quick agreement as suspect and will explore the reasons underlying our apparent agreement to make sure that our members have willingly agreed.

How Much Time Should This Take?

Consensus depends on allowing unlimited amounts of time to complete the process, so no time limit should be established. If the group members find they must take a break or reschedule the meeting to complete the process, be sure to summarize what has happened and review this summary at the beginning of the next session.

OBSERVING CONSENSUS

Time process started: ____________.

How did the facilitator explain the guidelines for reaching consensus?

Did the team members find out who had experience or knowledge in this topic?

Names **What was each member's stated position at the beginning?**

____

____

____

____

____

____

What methods were used by the facilitator to aid the team in reaching consensus? How successful were they?

What methods were used by the other team members to reach consensus? How successful were they?

How did members explain their points of view to the team?

Names **What was each member's stated position at the end?**

____

____

____

____

____

____

Do you think the team truly followed the guidelines for reaching consensus? Why or why not? Time process ended: ____________. Was this enough time to use this method successfully?

EVALUATION OF METHODS

After you have used one of these methods, evaluate how well it worked. This is especially important when you're trying out something new.

Use these questions for your self-evaluation:

______ Did the method or activity achieve the objective(s) I had for selecting it?

______ Did I give clear and concise directions?

______ Did I ask enough questions and were they directed appropriately?

______ Did I allow enough time for this activity?

______ Did this activity take place at the most appropriate time in the meeting?

______ How receptive were participants to this activity?

______ How could this method or activity be adapted for future use?

Chapter 7

Moving Beyond Problems to Action

INTRODUCTION

In this chapter you will learn how to go beyond problems by taking action with some problem solving models.

Most problem solving models go through a cycle as shown on the next page. The steps include naming the problem, analysing its causes, setting a goal, searching for alternative solutions, developing a plan and evaluating it after it is implemented.

For those simple problems your group or team wants to work on, use the Compact Problem Solving Method. It has five steps and takes about half an hour from naming the problem to evaluating the plan.

The Comprehensive Problem Solving Method is a very involved process. It initially evaluates a complex problem thoroughly and eventually results in a detailed plan of action. This method has six steps which take 3–5 hours to complete.

This chapter closes with an evaluation form that you can use to assess the effectiveness of the problem solving method you selected.

THE PROBLEM SOLVING CYCLE

The two problem solving methods described in this chapter include each part of this cycle.

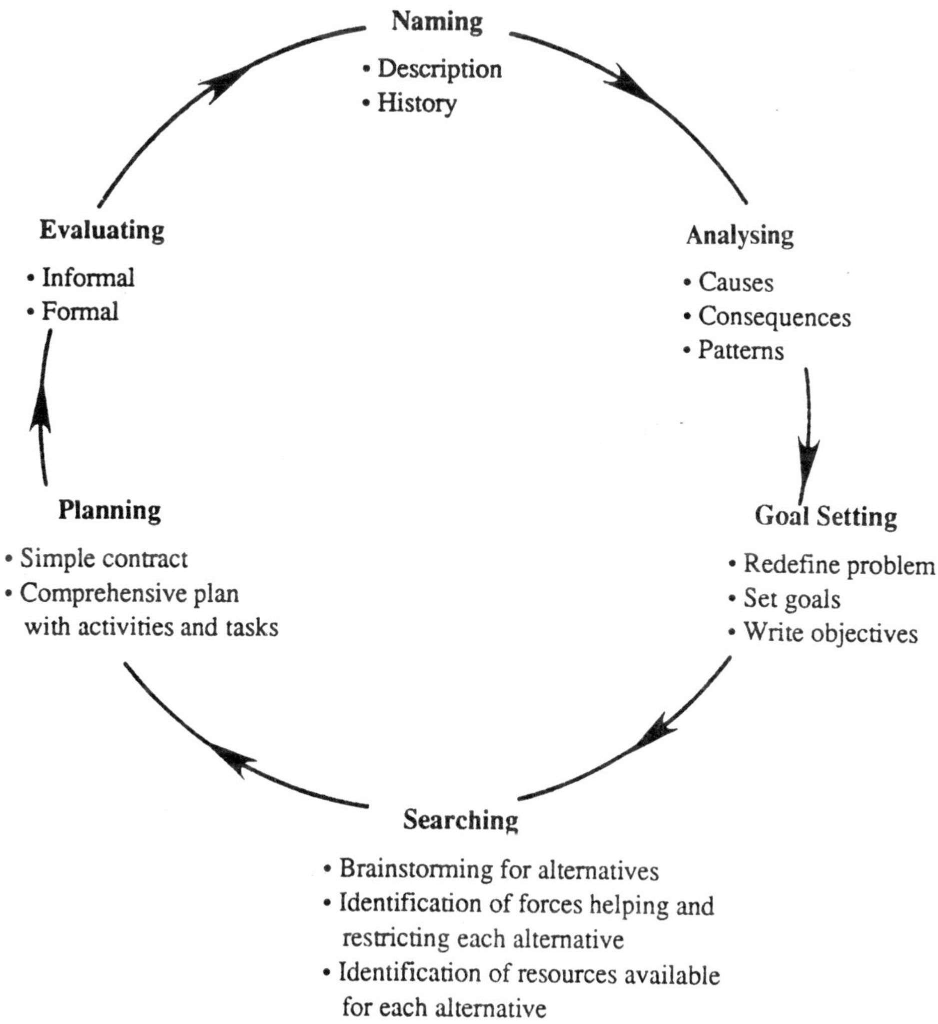

THE COMPACT PROBLEM SOLVING METHOD

The Compact Problem Solving Method is a quick process to evaluate a fairly simple problem and come up with some alternative solutions. The group size should be no smaller than three and no larger than eight.

The process has five timed steps taking about half an hour. It requires one person who is facing some problem to be the problem-poser while the remainder of the group asks clarifying questions, suggests solutions, and records statements.

Explain Purpose

Give the rationale for collaborative problem solving – a process by which a team of people work together, pooling their ideas and resources to find a solution to a problem.

Identify Problems

Identify problems that are relatively simple (see the Comprehensive Problem Solving Method for complex problems). Note which group members are facing each problem.

Arrange the Group

It is probably best to keep the group together through one problem unless there are more than eight people or if they are familiar with problem solving methods.

This process works well with groups of three, so after a demonstration the total group could be divided up according to a variety of problems. Each group *must* have at least three people because one person will be the problem-poser, one will serve as a recorder and one as a timer.

Group the members and arrange the chairs in a circle so everyone can easily hear and discuss ideas.

Overview of the Method

Review the following six steps so everyone knows what will be happening.

STEPS IN THE COMPACT PROBLEM SOLVING METHOD

Steps Required	Range of Time
1. Naming the Problem	5 minutes
2. Analysing	5 minutes
3. Goal Setting	5 minutes
4. Searching for Solutions	5 minutes
5. Planning	5–7 minutes
6. Evaluating	3–5 minutes

Step 1: Naming The Problem

The problem-poser takes no more than five minutes to describe a specific problem or incident to those in the group. These people listen carefully and avoid all talking except for clarification. Clarifying questions are asked by group members to assist the problem-poser in the description of the problem.

Description of Incident	1. Who was involved? What did each person say and do? 2. When and where does this problem usually occur?

History of Incident

1. Is there a prior history of this incident that makes it particularly problematic?
2. What related experiences in your life preceded the incident and set the stage for it? What occurred in the other person's life prior to the incident or problem?

Consequences

1. How did you feel during and after the incident?
2. How do you think the other person(s) felt?
3. What was the sequence of events and consequences just after the incident?

Step 2: Analysing

The next five minutes are spent analysing the problem in order to clarify what happened and why. The process encourages the problem-poser to be clearer about the desired outcome.

Down to Basics

The problem-poser completes each of these three sentences as many times as possible:

1. 'What I really wanted in this situation was . . .'
2. 'What the other person really wanted was . . .'
3. 'The basic conflict was . . .'

Unique or a Pattern?

To determine if the problem is unique or part of a recurring pattern, the problem-poser responds to these questions:

1. Has this incident occurred before? If so, have you and others reacted the same way?
2. Has this problem emerged for others in your organization?

Past Attempts It is helpful to identify practices regarding the problem.

1. What has been done in the past?
2. How did it work out?

Step 3: Goal Setting

The next five minutes are spent redefining the problem and determining the goal.

Goal Setting

1. What do you want to happen?
2. When would you know if your goals were achieved?

Step 4: Searching for Solutions

The next five minutes use the resources of all the members of the group in searching for alternative solutions to the problem described. The process used is brainstorming and requires the generation of many ideas in a very short period of time. Many people find this an enjoyable and useful experience.

Announce how much time will be used, alert the timer, and immediately solicit solutions.

To ensure a plethora of creative ideas, this problem solving method uses the pressure of a limited amount of time and the creation of a non-judgmental atmosphere, where all ideas are counted. The goal is to create ideas in quantity, regardless of quality.

To hold a brainstorming session, first introduce the group members to the purpose and steps of the process. Choose one person to record, as quickly as possible, all the ideas given by the group members. This can be done on a flipchart or ordinary paper. Abbreviations may be necessary in order to keep up with the group's suggestions. Write the problem on the flipchart or paper. Review the ground rules that all members must follow:

1. **Quantity, not quality.** Use the time to think of as many solutions as possible. The more bizarre, the better.

2. **Piggyback.** If someone else's idea triggers a slight variation of an idea for you, call it out.
3. **No evaluation.** All ideas are accepted. No judgment of ideas is allowed at this time. Do not stop to discuss the *pros* and *cons* of any suggestions.
4. **Stop immediately.** At the end of the five minutes, all brainstorming should end.

Step 5: Planning

In the fifth step, the problem-poser reviews all the alternatives suggested in order to select those solutions having the greatest potential. Using from five to seven minutes, the problem-poser evaluates each suggestion according to his or her own criteria, or the following:

1. **Impossible.** Eliminate those suggestions that are unrealistic or incompatible with your values or situation.
2. **Maybe.** Put an 'M' next to those you might consider.
3. **Outstanding.** Put an asterisk (*) next to those that strike you as creative, realistic or appealing.

The problem-poser and group members then discuss the most plausible solutions, refining the best ones to the point where the problem-poser believes they can work. From these, the problem-poser chooses at least one workable solution. A written plan is formalized by the problem-poser or recorder.

Step 6: Evaluating

In the last few minutes, the goal and plan are reviewed.

Too often, attempts to try something new can be lost in everyday routine or in the recurrence of a person's behavioural pattern. However, if the problem-poser commits himself or herself to a plan and combines this with support from the other members of the group, chances for success increase dramatically.

It is crucial, therefore, to indicate when, where, and how progress on the plan's implementation will be shared with the group members. Most likely, it can be reviewed at one of the next meetings or one member might phone to check.

During this follow-up the group as a whole can review the progress and perhaps make new suggestions if the problem-poser needs to modify the plan. This follow-up should take place fairly soon after the plan is developed, and should continue until the problem-poser has eliminated the problem.

THE COMPREHENSIVE PROBLEM SOLVING METHOD

The Comprehensive Problem Solving Method is a very involved process used to thoroughly evaluate a complex problem and come up with a detailed plan of action. The process has six steps that require three to five hours in total to complete.

Explain Purpose

Give the rationale for collaborative problem solving – a process by which a team of people work together, pooling their ideas and resources to find a solution to a problem.

Identify Problems

Identify problems that are relatively complex (use the Compact Problem Solving Method for simpler problems). Note which group members are facing each problem.

Arrange the Group

It is probably best to keep the group together during one problem unless they are quite familiar with problem solving methods.

Group the members around a table so that everyone can easily hear, discuss and take notes. Have a flipchart and markers available.

Overview of the Method

Review the following six steps so that everyone knows what will be happening and about how long each step will take.

STEPS IN THE COMPREHENSIVE PROBLEM SOLVING PROCESS

Steps	Range of Time Required	Work Sheets to Use
1. Naming the Problem	20–30 minutes	Naming the Problem
2. Analysing the Problem	10–20 minutes	Analysing the Problem
3. Goal Setting	10–15 minutes 25–35 minutes	A. Redefining the Problem B. Setting a Goal
4. Searching for Solutions	15–25 minutes 20–25 minutes 20–25 minutes 15–20 minutes	A. Brainstorming Strategies B. Force Field Analysis C. Evaluating Strategies D. Looking at Resources
5. Planning	20–30 minutes 20–30 minutes	Selecting Activities The Gantt Chart
6. Evaluating	15–30 minutes	
Total	3–5 hours	

Step 1: Naming The Problem

The goal of this first step is the development of a clear, concise statement of the problem; that is, the situation or condition considered to be undesirable. Because a problem statement often contains more than one problem, the process of clarification is the foundation of the entire process and is crucial to understanding the nature of the problem. Overlooking or rushing through this step affects all subsequent steps.

Allow 20–30 minutes for this part of the process.

If your group has more than one problem to solve, it may be best to list all perceived problems and then prioritize them according to their importance or immediacy. The group can decide which problems to deal with first, recognizing that other problems can be dealt with at a later date.

At this point, the process utilizes the first worksheet, 'Naming the Problem'. Each person completes the sheet and then shares her or his individual perceptions of the problem. The group reaches consensus on the problem, which is written on the flipchart.

WORKSHEET:

Step 1: Naming the Problem

Definition: A problem is a situation or condition considered to be undesirable.

Time: 20–30 minutes to complete and discuss.

Answer the following questions:

a. What is the problem?

b. Where is it a problem?

c. When is it a problem?

d. For whom is it a problem?

e. What is likely to happen in the future if something isn't done about the problem?

Problem Statement: Write your problem Statement:

Step 2: Analysing The Problem

This second step explores the causes and consequences resulting from the problem as described in the first step. Keep in mind these two definitions:

- A *cause* is what created the problem.
- A *consequence* is what is happening or may happen because of the problem.

The group members individually complete the second worksheet, 'Analysing the Problem', to gain further insight into the problem and potential solutions.

Next, the group discusses responses until reaching a consensus on the causes and consequences.

This step takes 10–20 minutes to complete the worksheet and reach consensus.

WORKSHEET:
Step 2: Analysing the Problem

Time: 10–20 minutes to complete and discuss.

List causes: A cause is what created the problem.

1.
2.
3.
4.
5.
6.

Which causes are the most significant?

Which causes will you attack (if any)?

List consequences: A consequence is what is happening or may happen because the problem exists.

1.
2.
3.
4.
5.
6.

Which consequences are the most undesirable?

Which consequences will you attack (if any)?

Step 3: Goal Setting

The third step is divided into two parts: redefinition of the problem and goal setting.

So far, the group has described the problem – its causes and consequences – so the problem is clearer. Now the group should be able to restate it in more specific terms. Using the third worksheet, 'Redefining the Problem', the group redefines the undesirable condition or situation. It also determines how it will benefit by resolving the described problem. This step will take 10–15 minutes.

After completing the new problem statement, the group focuses on identifying a desirable goal or outcome. Using the next worksheet, 'Setting a Goal', group members write a goal and set a deadline to accomplish it. The statement is reworked using the criteria that follow until they reach consensus. This will take 25–35 minutes.

Criteria	Means
Conceivable	capable of being put into words
Achievable	realistic in view of strengths, abilities, and present situation
Valuable	acceptable and compatible with our values
Manageable	dealing with only one goal at a time
Growth-facilitating	not harmful to us, others, or society

WORKSHEET:
Step 3A: Redefining the Problem

Definition: A problem is a situation or condition considered to be undesirable.

Time: 10–15 minutes

Self-interest: Record 'what's in it for us' statements about the problem.

Final problem statement: Restate the problem as clearly as possible.

WORKSHEET:

Step 3B: Setting a Goal

Definition: A goal is a situation or condition considered to be desirable.

Time: 25–35 minutes

Goal Statement:

Deadline: The goal will be accomplished by: ____________________

Criteria Check: Check the goal against the criteria: Is it?

Criteria	Yes	No	Maybe
Conceivable?			
Achievable?			
Valuable?			
Manageable?			
Growth-facilitating?			

Step 4: Searching For Solutions

This step has four parts that help the group think of alternative solutions to the defined problem and begin the process of selecting those that are most plausible:

1. Brainstorming Strategies
2. Applying Force Field Analysis
3. Evaluating Strategies
4. Identifying Resources

Brainstorming Strategies (15–25 minutes)

The first part in this step involves brainstorming, as described in Chapter 6. Be sure to review and follow the guidelines for using this method. The purpose, as before, is to generate a list of potential strategies.

A strategy is defined as a group of activities that are carried out to reach the goal. With the brainstorming method, the recorder lists all the ideas on the flipchart.

After 10–15 minutes (note that more time is allowed for the brainstorming portion in this comprehensive process), the group begins its evaluation of the suggestions on the list by marking each with the appropriate code:

If it is:	**Code:**
Impossible	Cross item out
Maybe	M
Outstanding	*

WORKSHEET:

Step 4A: Brainstorming Strategies

Definition: A strategy is a series or group of activities that are carried out to reach the goal.

Time: 15–25 minutes

Using the brainstorming technique, list your strategies below:

Strategies	**Code**
1.	
2.	
3.	
4.	
5.	
6.	
7.	
8.	
9.	
10.	

Applying Force Field Analysis (20–25 minutes)

Next, the group members apply the Force Field Analysis to a maximum of three of the most promising strategies. (Review this method in Chapter 6.)

Draw a Force Field Analysis chart for each of the three strategies chosen on which the helping and hindering forces affecting them are listed. Remember that the helping forces are those that work toward achievement of the goal and the hindering forces are those that work against it.

WORKSHEET:

Step 4B: Apply Force Field Analysis

Helping Forces →	← **Hindering Forces**

Evaluating Strategies (20–25 minutes)

Once the helping and hindering forces are listed, the group uses the questions below to help determine how to capitalize on the helping forces (increase them) and minimize the potency of the hindering forces (decrease them).

WORKSHEET:
Step 4C: Evaluating Strategies

1. Which forces can you influence?

2. How can the effects of the helping forces be increased?

3. How can the effects of the hindering forces be reduced?

4. What additional forces might be listed to help carry out the strategy?

Looking at Resources (15–20 minutes)

The last part of Step Four involves an analysis of the resources available to help solve the problem. This exercise frequently helps group members recognize the number and variety of resources available to them.

For each strategy still under discussion, use this worksheet. Resources can be tangible, such as people, money, equipment, facilities, as well as intangible, such as time, knowledge, skills, influence, prestige, and energy.

WORKSHEET:
Step 4D: Identifying Resources

Strategy: ______________________

Resource	**Is the resource needed for this strategy? Yes/No**	**Is the resource available? Yes/No**	**If not available, can the resource be obtained? Yes/No**
Personnel			
Money			
Equipment			
Premises			
Time			
Knowledge			
Skill			
Influence & Prestige			
Energy			

Step 5: Planning

The fifth step first involves breaking down the strategies into activities and then identifying tasks for carrying them out. This step is crucial to the success or failure of the problem solving effort and requires sincere commitment on the part of those involved. Each group member assumes ownership in the accomplishment of the goal by accepting responsibility for one or more of the identified activities.

Selecting Activities (20–30 minutes)

An activity is a specific procedure or process that is a part of an identified strategy. Use the 'Selecting Activities' worksheet to list activities that would be necessary to accomplish one strategy. Use the brainstorming method to generate a list of all possible activities.

WORKSHEET:
Step 5: Selecting Activities

Definition: An activity is a specific procedure or process that is part of a strategy for reaching the goal.

Strategy ______________________________

Activities: ______________________________

____

____

____

____

____

____

____

The Gantt Chart (20–30 minutes)

Next, this list of activities will be sorted out, deadlines set, and identification made of those who will be responsible for accomplishing each one.

Evaluate these activities, grouping them in the order by which they should be done. Use the Gantt Chart on the next page to list the activities in the approximate order in which they will be done under the 'What' column.

Next, identify who will be responsible for accomplishing each activity. In the column marked 'Who', write the name or initials of the person(s) responsible. Each person may assume responsibility for one major activity, as well as assisting in many tasks. Such teamwork is not only desirable, but necessary.

Add a deadline for each activity in the 'When' column.

The vertical columns are for dates covering 21 days. Select your starting day and enter it on the first vertical column, and label each column with sequential dates.

Opposite each activity, put the letter 'S' in the column for its start date and the letter 'C' for the projected date of completion. Draw a horizontal line from the 'C' to the 'S', which covers the period of time you've identified to complete that activity.

Use the Gantt Chart to monitor the group's progress on the activities. Use a different coloured pen to mark the planned dates and what really happens. If more time is needed, put a dash (—) on the line showing the new deadline. Be sure to keep this chart updated at least weekly. Obviously, the chart is useless if left in a drawer or file; keep it handy for periodic review.

Gantt Chart

WHAT	WHO	WHEN											

Step 6: Evaluating

Your role as facilitator also includes responsibility for monitoring the plan. You must be sure that the problem statement, goal, strategies, activities and Gantt Chart are collected, edited, and retyped, and that copies are distributed so that everyone knows his or her part in the plan. Knowing one's responsibilities reduces misunderstandings and improves accountability, both of which are crucial to successful implementation of the plan.

Now that the planning step is complete, lead the group in an evaluation of the Comprehensive Problem Solving Process. Plan on 15–30 minutes for this step. You might discuss some of these questions:

1. How did you feel before, during, and after using the model?
2. What was the most useful part? Least useful?
3. What variables would have made the process more constructive?
4. How can we use this process in the future? When should we do it again? What changes need to be made?

EVALUATION OF METHODS

After you have used one of these methods, evaluate how well it worked. This is especially important when you're trying out something new.

Use these questions for your self-evaluation:

______ Did the method or activity achieve the objective(s) I had for selecting it?

______ Did I give clear and concise directions?

______ Did I ask enough questions and were they directed appropriately?

______ Did I allow enough time for this activity?

______ Was this activity in the most appropriate place in the meeting?

______ How receptive were participants to this activity?

______ How could this method or activity be adapted for future use?

Chapter 8

Supporting Facilitation with Visual Aids

INTRODUCTION

A group or team's activities are often enhanced by the use of flipcharts, transparencies, videos or films. In addition, visual aids may be used in presentations made to others.

Visual aids and other resources should be used when appropriate and not just as fillers or for entertainment. It is important to think about what purpose any of these will serve. Here are some examples:

- A flipchart or transparency can help focus attention on what is being discussed and serve as a summary.
- A video or film can increase interest in the topic and also provide useful background information.
- These visual aids engage more than one of our senses, which enhances learning.

In this chapter, you will find guidelines on how to record information using flipcharts and marking pens and an outline on the impact of using different colours.

You will also find information on how to prepare transparencies that are both readable and appealing.

When you have a use for a video film, review the four steps listed in this chapter.

RECORDING WITH FLIPCHARTS, EASELS AND MARKING PENS

Flipcharts are frequently used in group meetings for recording ideas, solutions, and decisions. The essential equipment consists of an easel to which is attached an A1 pad of blank paper on which information will be recorded with felt tip markers.

There are certain general guidelines that ensure that your flipcharts are readable and useful to the group members.

Guidelines

- Position the flipchart so that everyone can see it. Walk to different areas in the room to check for readability. Make sure the easel's legs are firmly positioned.
- Stand at an angle to the easel as you write and then stand to the side while listening to the next speaker.
- Use paper that has faint lines on it so that you write straight.
- Write in large block letters at least $1\frac{1}{2}$ inches high.
- Leave 2 inches or more between lines.
- Use several coloured marking pens.
- Use as few words as possible.
- Abbreviate words and use symbols, but make sure the group understands them.

- Highlight key words with:
  - circles
  - boxes
  - underlining
  - arrows
  - pictures
  - contrasting colour
- If you aren't sure how to spell a word and you feel everyone's eyes on your back, perhaps ask for help.
- Write a maximum of 10 lines per sheet of paper.
- Write on only the top two-thirds of the sheet.
- As a sheet is full, tear it off and post it on a wall. Ask someone else to help you with this task.

IF . . .	THEN . . .
• You are recording the group's input	• Record key words quickly. • Check with contributors to be sure you are reflecting their ideas accurately.
• You wish them to compare and contrast data	• Use two flipcharts.
• You want to display information for a period of time	• Hang pages on the wall with masking tape.
• You don't have an easel	• Post a large piece of paper on a wall but put a blank piece behind it to avoid the ink bleeding through.
• You want to prerecord information	• Leave a blank page between sheets to avoid bleed-through and distraction.
• You want to look especially professional in front of the group	• Lightly write memory joggers in pencil in margin of flipchart page. • Practise tearing pages cleanly before trying it in front of the group. • Cover flipchart information when not in use.

Colour Makes a Difference!

Colour can be used to stimulate or to calm, to enhance or to distract. Colours carry special meanings, so become familiar with these associations and select colours that relate to the recorded content.

Colour	Associations	Impact on participants
Black	neutral, basic	depressing, suggests the unknown or concealment
White	pure and clean	suggests frankness and revelation
These three colours fall into the family of cool colours:		
Blue	sky, water	thoughtful; suggests knowledge; calms the mind; promotes creativity
Green	nature, growth	suggests harmony, peace and balance; heals, restores and fosters compassion
Purple	spiritual, dignified	status; power; healing; inspiration
These three colours fall into the family of warm colours:		
Yellow	sunlight, warmth	cheerful, inspiring, and joyful; helps digestion of ideas
Red	fire, hot	passionate; exciting; active colour of life; stimulates activity
Orange	autumn	lively; forceful; courage and stamina useful for positive thinking

USING TRANSPARENCIES FOR GIVING OVERVIEWS

Transparencies are acetate sheets containing information and are used with an overhead projector. The image is shown on a screen or blank wall.

Like the flipchart, transparencies can help focus attention on what is being discussed. They can also provide useful background information.

As a visual aid, transparencies have special advantages, but they also have significant drawbacks if not used properly.

ADVANTAGES	DRAWBACKS
+ Add a professional touch	– Light and glare can be tiring if overused
+ Easily transported	– Require special equipment not always readily available
+ Can use with large audience (over 25)	– Complex charts can overwhelm viewers

As with flipcharts, you can develop transparencies ahead of time or develop them during the meeting. If you decide to develop transparencies in advance of your meeting, there are two ways to do so:

1. Professionally

   Graphic artists can professionally produce your transparencies. You will need to provide the information.

2. Personally

   a. Prepare the information on paper and have it copied onto a sheet of acetate using a copying machine.
   b. Make a transparency by using transparency markers directly onto the acetate.

Guidelines for Making Transparencies Readable and Appealing

Regardless of whether you are making the transparency yourself, or supplying the information for an artist to make your transparency, there are guidelines to ensure that your transparencies are readable and appealing to group members.

- Include one major idea, with up to three subpoints, on each transparency.
- Use as few words as possible to communicate your ideas.
- Keep information to six lines or less, with no more than six words per line.
- Use coloured acetate to reduce the glare and provide variety.
- Illustrate ideas with:

  Pictures
  Shapes
  Graphs
  Colour

- Use a grid to ensure straight lines.

Transparency Tips

IF . . .	THEN . . .
• You are using more than one transparency	• Turn projector on, show a transparency, then turn it off – unless you are showing a series in rapid succession. • Don't keep a transparency on too long. The image becomes tiring for viewers.

• You want the group to focus on a specific area	• Try one of these methods: Use a pencil or a pointer to accent the area. Reveal one area at a time by using a paper to 'mask' the area you don't want to show. Place the paper between the transparency and the glass for extra control and to enable you to read the masked information.
• You are using the same transparencies in subsequent sessions	• Use permanent marking pens. • Mount transparencies in frames to keep them from curling. • Store them sandwiched between papers in a dust-free location.
• You wish to change the information	Use water-soluble marking pens. Run water or a damp cloth over the area to remove the ink.
• You want to appear more professional in front of the group	• Write memory joggers in black ink on the transparency frames and use them as your presentation notes. • Place masking tape around the edges of the projector glass to keep out the projection light and keep the framed transparencies from slipping.

USING VIDEOTAPES AND FILMS FOR BACKGROUND INFORMATION

Videotapes and films add a great deal to a team's activities. These two visual aids help to stimulate interest and motivation. The content can provide illustrations and models for the ideas and skills you are discussing in your group.

Steps For Using a Videotape/Film

If you decide to use a videotape or film, follow these four steps:

STEP 1: Prepare for showing.	• Check that the videotape or film is the correct size for the available equipment. • Preview and identify the important points you want group members to take in from viewing the videotape or film. • Test the equipment and check lighting levels. If you will be asking the group members to take notes, adjust lighting plans accordingly.
STEP 2: Provide instructions.	• Give participants an overview of what they will see and why this is being presented. • Instruct the group on what to do during the viewing. Take notes or watch for certain examples. • Tell them what they will do after the film or videotape is over.

STEP 3: Play the videotape/film.	• Adjust lighting. • Start video/film and adjust picture and volume. • Monitor reactions to the video/film.
STEP 4: Discuss and summarize major points.	• At the end of the videotape/film, have a discussion of the group's reactions. • Summarize the key points you want group members to retain from the videotape/film.

Chapter 9

Keeping People Informed

INTRODUCTION

Most teams function within an organizational structure and thus are accountable to others. As the facilitator of a team, you will need to keep certain people in the organization informed about what the team is doing at different points in their process.

Three groups of people need to be informed: the members of the team, the supervisor to whom the team is accountable, and other managers.

The members of the team you are facilitating need to have some method of keeping a record of what they are doing. This serves two purposes: to provide an historical record they can refer to and to update members who either missed meetings or joined the team later on. This chapter contains a sample group memo form for recording what happened during the meetings. Your organization may have some forms currently in use that would also work well.

You probably need to report to a particular boss or bosses who hold some responsibility for the team's results. Your team may think they only need to submit a report when the end results are clear; however, instead you probably need to give status reports at least once during the process. A guideline used in some organizations is to expect to give two status reports and one final report within eight weeks. The boss may need this information before the final report is available.

You possibly know how frustrating it is to put in many hours on a project only to find out that the results are not what the boss had in mind. These periodic updates or status reports help to clarify the original assignment and ensure that you are headed in the right direction.

You can use the Group Memo or Status Report forms found in this chapter. The key is to find out how often the boss wants information and in what form.

Most teams are required to produce a final report of some kind. Although your team may need to provide a written report, often you or the team members will need to make a formal presentation to upper management or to employees on your recommendations for changes in policies and procedures.

Written reports or presentations can be either an overview of the results or a more detailed report. Giving presentations requires careful planning. This chapter outlines six steps for preparing a presentation.

PREPARING A GROUP MEMO

After the meeting is over, most groups need a written record of what happened at the meeting, what decisions were made and what the next steps will be. The facilitator or recorder uses the notes taken at the meeting to develop a short but useful group memo that is then distributed to those who attended. This can help update those who were absent and those who should be kept informed of the group's progress.

The outline of a group memo follows on the next page:

NAME: ______ TOPIC/TITLE: ______ DATE: ______		
What Happened/Group Process Used:		
Decisions/Action Items:	**Person Responsible for Action:**	**By When?**
Next Steps:		
This group memo is my interpretation of what happened at this meeting. Please let me know if there's an error. For more information concerning any details of the meeting, feel free to call me. Recorder ______________		

This is an example of a group memo completed after a meeting:

NAME: Executive Staff TOPIC/TITLE: Budget Cuts DATE: 5/2/91

What Happened/Group Process Used:

Sally met with the five Division Directors to review the reasons for the forthcoming budget cuts and the amount needing cutting. After answering general questions, we split into groups to brainstorm areas that might be trimmed in the budget. In the total group, the ideas were grouped by type on the flipchart. (See the attached list of ideas.)

We decided to replicate this process with each of our divisional staffs so they will be committed to this team problem of cutting the budget.

Joe agreed to review sources of cost cutting with our three major suppliers and to invite them to our next meeting.

Decisions/Action Items:	Person Responsible for Action:	By When?
1. Use this process with each member of division staff; generate list of ideas and compare to Executive Staff's	Division Directors	10/2/91
2. Review cost cutting ideas with our three major suppliers	Joe	15/2/91

Next Steps:

The Executive staff will meet at 10:00 AM on Friday, February 15 to review the lists generated by the employees and discuss ideas with suppliers. We will then rank the ideas.

This group memo is my interpretation of what happened at this meeting. Please let me know if there's an error. For more information concerning any details of the meeting, feel free to call me.

Recorder Dave Smith

PREPARING A STATUS REPORT

Periodically, you may need to submit a status report to the boss who wants to know your progress, preliminary decisions and problems. The recorder or facilitator uses information gathered in meetings and documented on their group memos to compile this status report.

The outline of a Status Report looks like this:

PROJECT NAME: ______________________ **DATE:** __________ PROGRESS SINCE LAST REPORT:
CURRENT STATUS:
PROBLEMS:
FACILITATOR ____________________

MAKING A PRESENTATION

There will probably be occasions when you will need to make a presentation to your boss or other managers. They often want to be kept informed about your group's activities, its progress, and how they might help. Therefore, it is important to know how to prepare a presentation.

You also might need to make a presentation to your team members so they have the same background information. For instance, you may need to prepare an historical overview of why Total Quality Management (TQM) is being introduced into your company, key concepts of TQM, and how teams will function. Or perhaps your organization is concerned about customer service, so you might need to do some research and present an overview of what the current literature says about how to have a successful customer service programme.

DIFFERENCES BETWEEN FACILITATION AND GIVING A PRESENTATION

	FACILITATION	PRESENTATIONS
Purpose:	• To lead a group in its discussion • To acomplish a task or solve a problem	• To inform, report, instruct, motivate, or entertain
Relationship to Group Members:	The facilitator encourages members to participate fully and interact with one another continually.	Usually the presentation is completed and then questions are asked.
Size of Group:	Ideally 6–15	Any size

SIMILARITIES BETWEEN FACILITATION AND GIVING A PRESENTATION

- The facilitator and presenter must be well prepared and thoroughly versed in the topics covered.
- Knowledge of the group members is needed.
- A presenter needs to know how to handle questions as much as a facilitator would; however, the facilitator would ask questions of the group members as well as answer their questions.

Six Steps in Preparing for a Presentation

There are six steps in preparing for a presentation:

1. Determine your objectives for the presentation.
2. Analyse your audience.
3. Prepare a preliminary outline.
4. Select and/or prepare visual aids.
5. Finalize the presentation outline with details.
6. Practise!

STEP 1: Determine your objectives for the presentation

In order to determine your objectives for giving this presentation, answer the following questions:

- Who suggested that this should be done? (You? Your boss?)
- When and where will it happen?
- Is your presentation a part of a longer design? If yes, what precedes or follows yours?
- How much do you know about the topic?
- Should the presentation be technical, theoretical, or practical?
- Why are you giving this presentation?

Write a short goal statement that outlines the purpose of the presentation.

STEP 2: Analyse your audience

The second step requires you to analyse your audience so the presentation can be geared to them. In order to do this, answer these questions:

- How much do they already know about your topic?
- What is their attitude towards the topic? (Hostile? Approving?)
- Why are they attending this presentation? (Volunteer? Mandatory?)
- What is their level of vocabulary relative to what you will present?
- How open-minded are they? (Eager? Neutral? Resistant?)
- What are some presentation techniques that might gain their attention?
- What are some presentation techniques that might get negative reactions from them?

STEP 3: Prepare a preliminary outline

You are now ready to prepare a preliminary outline based on what you know about the participants.

Outline the main ideas you want to convey first. Consider putting each main idea on a separate slip of paper. After you've listed them, arrange the slips in an approximate order for presentation. At this point, you could type out your preliminary outline.

Add notes on ideas or examples that would support each main idea.

STEP 4: Select and/or prepare visual aids

For each main idea, think about using visual aids that could present the information more clearly or would support what you will be presenting.

Which form of visual aid can you supply and would be best to use?

Video Film Flipcharts Transparencies Handouts

STEP 5: Finalize the presentation outline with details

Now you are ready to finalize your outline. First make sure that your points are in a logical order. Indicate in your notes where you will use your visual aids (you could use a symbol). Also indicate on your outline where you are willing to pause and answer questions.

Next determine how you will introduce your presentation. Some choices include:

- Direct statement of what will be presented and why it is important to your audience
- Indirect opening using something that is of vital interest to your audience and would lead into your topic
- Vivid example or comparison that leads into your topic
- A strong quotation that relates to your topic
- Important statistics
- A story that illustrates what you are about to say.

Last, plan how you will summarize and close your presentation. It is important to restate your main ideas. End with a positive, direct appeal for action or vividly review the purpose of your presentation. Sometimes a final example, quotation or story works well.

STEP 6: Practise! Practise! Practise!

Chapter 10

Evaluating and Ending Your Group or Team

INTRODUCTION

This final chapter covers how to evaluate your team's progress both while still together and when they are about to disband. There are some forms included that will help you in this evaluation process.

You have learned the value of warm-up activities used to build interpersonal relationships and trust. It is just as valuable to end your team's experience with some structured activities. This chapter contains some examples for you.

You may also want the team members to stay in contact, so there are some follow-up ideas included.

After your team responsibilities are finished, you should do a self-evaluation on how you feel you did as their facilitator, what you did well, and what you would do differently the next time you are a facilitator.

This chapter has another self-assessment form for you to complete to help you identify what skills and methods you now feel competent to use. Compare this assessment with the one you completed earlier.

This book concludes with information on how to decide if you are ready to facilitate alone or if you would prefer to co-facilitate. Team facilitating can be fun! If you choose to try this route, you will find some guidelines that will help you work as part of a team.

EVALUATION

Evaluating your group's progress is important so that you can determine what worked and what didn't. This evaluation can be done very informally with a few questions or more formally with an instrument. What is more important than how you evaluate your group is that it is done both while the group is together and also when it disbands.

There are many reasons why a group may temporarily stop meeting or disband completely. Most groups meet over a period of time and not just for one session. However, other demands on their time may require holding infrequent meetings. In other cases, group members may need to do research or developmental work before the group can proceed with its plans. Therefore, a gap of several weeks or even months may pass between their getting together.

Some groups meet for a particular purpose, accomplish their goal and disband, probably never to regroup again. In each case, the team members need to tie up some loose ends before leaving one another, even temporarily.

There are many activities that help the group members focus on what they learned from each other and what individual goals they have for follow-up. There are also methods for evaluating the progress and accomplishment of the group.

Many groups want to stay in touch, so use follow-up ideas on how the group members can do that with each other and the facilitator.

On the following pages, you will see examples of how to evaluate and complete your group's experience.

EVALUATING YOUR GROUP

Periodically, it is useful to evaluate how well the group is functioning. This information can help you and the team to modify activities, resolve conflicts, use time better or solve problems differently.

Initially, you might want to use an evaluation form that is completed anonymously by each person. You can summarize the answers and report this to the group. You can also indicate how you plan to incorporate their suggestions into the group's process. The members can also discuss changes they will make in their behaviour.

The first example of an evaluation form, shown on the next page, uses a scale of one to five whereas the second example asks open-ended questions. Review these two examples to determine whether the questions fit what you know about your group and how they've been working together. Then adapt these forms to fit your needs.

By administering these forms periodically, you and the group can see the progress you are making. Over time, you and the team will become comfortable with one another and you can skip using a form by holding a discussion to evaluate your progress.

Here is a list of categories you might use when evaluating the group's progress, either on a form or in a discussion. Be sure to ask a variety of questions.

______ Goals
______ Procedures and ground rules
______ Productivity
______ Roles
______ Participation by members
______ Level of commitment
______ Level of interest
______ Communication patterns
______ General atmosphere
______ Conflicts
______ Facilitation
______ Timing
______ Trust
______ Synergy
______ Feelings
______ Problem solving methods
______ Other activities

HOW WELL ARE WE WORKING TOGETHER?

We have been working together as a team for quite a while. It is time to step back and evaluate both our relationships with one another and progress on our goals. You do not need to sign this form. I will summarize the results and review them with you at the next meeting.

Circle the number on each scale that identifies how well you think our team has been working together. Feel free to add any comments.

Goals

1 2 3 4 5

None set or irrelevant — Well defined and clear goals

Commitment

1 2 3 4 5

Individuals protect self-interest — Individuals support each other and group's goals

Procedures & Guidelines

1 2 3 4 5

Unclear or not followed — Clearly agreed upon and followed

Roles

1 2 3 4 5

Roles are rigid — We rotate roles

Participation

1 2 3 4 5

Few people are involved — Everyone is involved and eager to participate

Trust

1 2 3 4 5

Very low trust — High level of trust

Conflict

1 2 3 4 5

Little evidence — High level of conflicts

Hidden Agendas

1 2 3 4 5

Great deal seems hidden; unresolved conflicts — None, everything is on the table

Timing

1 2 3 4 5

Much wasted time — Time well spent

Facilitation

1 2 3 4 5

Inappropriate amount of direction and control — Just the right amount of direction and control

HOW WELL ARE WE WORKING TOGETHER?

We have been working together as a team for quite a while. It is time to step back and evaluate how we are doing. You do not need to sign this. I will summarize the results and review them with you at the next meeting.

1. How did you feel when we first formed this team?

2. How do you feel now?

3. Which of this team's goals do you think we've achieved?

4. What unresolved conflicts do you think this team needs to address?

5. What prevents you from being more committed, interested or participating more?

6. With whom do you feel most comfortable?

7. Who, if anyone, is a problem for you in this group?

8. How can the facilitator help this group move forward?

9. What additional ground rules or procedures do you wish this group would use?

ENDING YOUR GROUP'S OR TEAM'S EXPERIENCE

Ending your group's or team's experience is just as essential as starting it off right. As the facilitator you need to plan for some meaningful activities that can be used periodically at the end of sessions and others that can be used when the group disbands altogether.

The following activities are just a few selected from *Saying Goodbye: Ending Your Group Experience*. They meet two objectives:

1. To help the group members share their perceptions of one another as working colleagues, and
2. To help them reflect on what they've gained from this team experience and determine what personal goals they want to put into action.

There are many more activities available in other books on the market. You might want to start a file of additional ideas so that you have a variety to meet different needs.

Saying Goodbye: Ending Your Group Experience by Lois B. Hart (Leadership Dynamics, 875 Poplar Ave., Boulder, CO 80304).

Sharing Positive Feedback

GOAL: To provide an opportunity for members to share some positive feedback about each other.

ESTIMATED TIME: 5–10 minutes

STEP 1: Introduce this activity with the fact that we often work together on tasks and neglect to tell each other what we like about being together.

Ask the members to silently scan the faces of the others and think about what they appreciate about each person.

STEP 2: Each person is then the focus of attention while the other group members give him/her some positive feedback.

After receiving several comments, each individual then shares what they liked about his/her behaviour or contributions during this group or team experience.

STEP 3: Continue until each person, including the facilitator, receives positive feedback from the others.

Last Time Around the Circle

GOAL: To give members the chance to compare their current expectations with what they originally wanted from this group or team experience.

ESTIMATED TIME: 5–10 minutes

STEP 1: Explain that we all brought along some expectations when we first joined this new group or team.

STEP 2: Ask each person to silently think of the expectation that he/she had originally and if it was met.

STEP 3: Either in sequential or random order, ask each person to briefly restate his/her earlier expectation and what he/she feels was gained.

VARIATIONS: Use a different topic for sharing such as:

'One goal we achieved that pleased me was . . .'

'Something I contributed to this group/team was . . .'

'I liked working in this group/team because . . .'

Live and Learn

GOAL: To help members reflect upon what they learned by being in this group or team experience.

ESTIMATED TIME: 10–15 minutes

STEP 1: Suggest that in everything we do, we have the opportunity to learn something new about ourselves. Give examples.

STEP 2: Make copies of the following either as a handout or on a flipchart and ask each person to complete one or more of the sentences:

> ***DIRECTIONS:*** Reflect upon your experience working in this group/team and decide what you learned about yourself by completing one or more of the following:
>
> I learned that . . .
>
> I was proud that I . . .
>
> I was surprised when . . .
>
> I was disappointed that I . . .
>
> Next time, I would . . .

STEP 3: Ask for volunteers to share what they wrote.

FOLLOW-UP IDEAS

Eventually, most groups accomplish their goals and disband. However, the members may want to keep in contact with one another and with you. As their facilitator, you may want to use some of these follow-up ideas to keep in touch with them, and to provide additional support and resources.

- Provide a list of all group members' names, addresses and phone numbers. Periodically update this information.
- Give the participants your phone number and encourage them to call you.
- Call them periodically and see if they have any problems or successes.
- Send a follow-up questionnaire that helps participants identify the areas that they might want to develop or for which they need resources.
- Add them to your mailing list so they will receive resources that you know might help them.
- Give them a subscription to a magazine or newsletter that provides resources they could use.
- Invite them to events that might reinforce and extend what they need to know.
- Plan a reunion.

HOW WELL ARE YOU DOING AS A FACILITATOR?

The purpose of this follow-up assessment is for you to review your progress as a facilitator, what skills you now possess and those you need to develop further.

1. EXPERIENCE AS A FACILITATOR: List a recent experience you had as a facilitator of any group.

2. MOTIVATION: Compare how you felt as you started out with this group to how you feel now. Has your motivation increased or diminished?

3. CHALLENGES: What was most difficult for you as the facilitator?

4. ACCOMPLISHMENTS: What went well for you?

The following is a list of facilitation skills and methods that were presented in this book. Read over this list and rate your current level of competence and confidence in the appropriate column. Turn back to your original self-assessment on page 12, record the number in the left column, then record the difference.

1 = I have no knowledge or experience in this area.
2 = I have some knowledge or experience in this area.
3 = I can do this at an average level of competency.
4 = I am confident in this area.
5 = I feel competent and confident enough to teach someone else.

Before	Now	Difference	
____	____	____	The difference between leading, training, and facilitating
____	____	____	The role of the facilitator
____	____	____	Roles people play in groups and teams
____	____	____	Handling problem people
____	____	____	The role of the recorder
____	____	____	The role of a process observer
____	____	____	How to use outside resource people
____	____	____	Setting up arrangements for a group meeting
____	____	____	How to warm-up a group or team and get them started
____	____	____	How to get a group or team to make a commitment
____	____	____	Guidelines for giving feedback
____	____	____	How adults work together
____	____	____	Observation of non-verbal signals
____	____	____	Listening and paraphrasing
____	____	____	Asking questions
____	____	____	Mediating conflicts between people
____	____	____	How to regroup creatively
____	____	____	Determining timing

Before	Now	Difference	
____	____	____	How to keep energy flowing
____	____	____	Using the brainstorming technique
____	____	____	Using the nominal grouping technique
____	____	____	Using a force field analysis
____	____	____	How to reach consensus
____	____	____	How to use the problem solving method
____	____	____	How to use a flipchart
____	____	____	How to use a videotape or film
____	____	____	How to use transparencies
____	____	____	How to prepare a presentation
____	____	____	How to write summary reports
____	____	____	Ending the group's or team's experience
____	____	____	Evaluating how well the group or team worked together

SHOULD YOU FACILITATE ALONE?

Now that you've completed your self-assessment, you know those strengths that you possess that will help you to be a facilitator and you'vc identified those areas that still need development.

You have probably thought about whether or not you want or need to team up with someone else in the facilitation role.

There is a value in team facilitating, but only if it meets your needs. For instance, if you have mostly '5s' on your self-assessment, you probably will want to go solo as a facilitator. But if you marked many items with a '1' or '2', consider co-facilating.

Here are some reasons you might want to team up with others:

1. You don't know enough! You need someone else because he or she would add a special expertise or perspective that perhaps you don't have. Perhaps you don't know how to use some of the problem solving methods such as consensus and could team up with someone who does. Or perhaps you don't have experience working with particular types of people, such as production supervisors.

2. You don't feel very confident. We all have times when we just don't feel confident enough to do a job alone. Then team up with someone who does!

   Those areas you identified with '2–4' on your self-assessment are the ones you need to practise more and often it is easier to do this with someone else.

3. You need to share a resource. People team up because they need to share meeting space, equipment or other resources.

4. You are lazy and don't want to do all that work alone. Yes, that's a valid reason to team up with someone else, because often the joint effort can energize you both.

5. It's more fun as a team. Why do this if it's not going to be fun?

If you have decided to team up with another facilitator, use these guidelines to help you work well together:

1. Decide why you want to do this together.
2. Get to know each other, your experiences, philosophy, knowledge and skills. Share your strengths and weaknesses. Set some goals for your professional development so you can help each other obtain them.
3. Outline any tasks that need to be done and who will do them – with deadlines. With this outlined, you are able to do some work separately knowing that your partner is doing his/her part.
4. Plan to work together respecting each other's energy levels and other commitments. Often one of you will work better in the morning and the other in the afternoon. Teammates will also have other commitments that must be respected, so discuss these obligations and deadlines so you won't be disappointed or frustrated with one another.
5. Determine how to pay for any expenses. Often there are expenses that may or may not be reimbursed. Decide who will pay for the typist, copies, computer costs or supplies. Keep a ledger and correct inequities periodically.
6. Deal with ego and conflict issues. Find out each other's sensitive points so they can be respected. Since conflicts will arise, discuss in advance how you will resolve them.
7. Let the woman go first when facilitating. No, this isn't because of etiquette, it's because of credibility. We have consistently found that participants accept the woman facilitator more readily if she starts off the process and, of course, shares equally in the facilitation.
8. Present yourselves as a team. As you discuss your plans with others, use the inclusive 'we' so that you, and others, perceive you as a team.
9. Plan a celebration! When your team has accomplished its goal or one of you withdraws from team facilitation, have a celebration. Evaluate what worked and what didn't, so that next time you consider team facilitating you'll say, 'Yes, let's team up as facilitators!'

Chapter 11

Summary

YOU'RE NOW A FAULTLESS FACILITATOR!

Now that you have worked your way through this book, you realize how much you know about facilitation:

- You now understand the difference between a group and a team.
- You know which key attitudes and behaviours you need to demonstrate in order to be an effective facilitator.
- You have observed the roles that members play and those behaviours that help or hinder the team's process.
- You know about the administrative details that must be coordinated, which will make the members' experience comfortable.
- You recognize the value of applying the adult learning principles.
- You know how to warm-up and end your group's experience.
- You have helped teams establish and follow their own guidelines.
- You have learned some communication and conflict resolution skills.
- You have learned how to trust your instincts and utilize energizers.
- You know the problem solving cycle and have many problem solving and decision-making methods you can use.
- You have tips on using visual aids and ways to report to others on your team's progress.

Now that's a lot of learning!

This book is a comprehensive resource book and by now you should be quite familiar with the book's organization to know where to find what you need.

Remember that there are no absolutes – what works in one circumstance may not work in another. Experiment and take some risks to see what works. Take notes on what does work and what you'd do differently next time. Adapt methods and ideas to fit your style and the needs of your team. Add other useful information from other sources. Remember that *Faultless Facilitation* is your tool to help you enjoy facilitating teams.

You're now a Faultless Facilitator!